REDISCOVERING

OUR HOLINESS HERITAGE

How The Wesleyan Church
Can Get Back What We Gave Away

REDISCOVERING

OUR HOLINESS HERITAGE

How The Wesleyan Church
Can Get Back What We Gave Away

Daniel E. LeRoy

Old Blue Truck Publishing Co.

708 Tar Heel Trail   Kernersville, North Carolina   27284

Old Blue Truck Publishing Co.
708 Tar Heel Trail
Kernersville, North Carolina 27284

Old Blue Truck Publishing Co. is the self-publishing ministry of Daniel E. LeRoy.
pastordan@ncewesleyan.com   (336) 813-5494

Special assistance provided by Timothy Kirkpatrick, **SECOND CHAIR** SOLUTIONS,
www.secondchair.church   (337) 281-5687

Cover Design: Daniel E. LeRoy

ISBN 9781729228456

Printed in the United States of America

True holiness is a witness that cannot be ignored.
Real sainthood is a phenomenon to which even the skeptic pays tribute.
The power of a life where Christ is exalted
would arrest and subdue those who are bored to tears
by our thin version of Christianity.

– Albert Day

CONTENTS

DISCLAIMER

This book is published as a service to The Wesleyan Church
and as a challenge for The Wesleyan Church. The views expressed in this
book are the views of the author and not necessarily those of
The Wesleyan Church.

You will not – nor should you – agree with everything in this book. It is
not a history textbook. It is a book of opinion based on history. But you
should not dismiss it without wrestling through these issues and the claims
of the Holy Spirit on your heart and life.

I pray it will renew a fire among us that will burn down our religion,
burn through racial barriers, and burn up our prideful self-righteousness
as it roars into a flame that cannot be contained, and bursts forth in a
roaring inferno of holy love, for the Glory of God and the eternal good of
the lost, the littlest, the least and the last.

– Pastor Dan

Dedication

This book is dedicated to my holiness preacher dad, Daniel Edwin LeRoy.

His family attended the Mead Memorial Methodist Church (M.E. South) in Russell, Kentucky, but it didn't really take with him. He was content to be a nominal Methodist until he met that holiness girl, Christyna Wihelmina Fosson, in high school. He was an All-State basketball player. She was a Homecoming Queen. He taught her how to jitterbug, much to the chagrin of her parents, and she tamed him and introduced him to Jesus, much to the relief of his parents.

They became active in the Westwood Christian Baptist Church of God of the Ohio River Valley, a part of a small holiness denomination of Free Will Baptists that had discovered holiness and got invited to leave.

They were enthusiastic youth workers and active church members. On his thirtieth birthday, in the wee hours of the morning, God called him to preach. He never looked back.

The Christian Baptist Church only had two or three fulltime works. It was part of their DNA. He served as a bi-vocational pastor in two churches, but yearned to be in ministry fulltime. Offers came to them from the Methodist Church in Kentucky, but it was their friendship with Pilgrim Holiness evangelist P.O. Carpenter that God used to open the door for them into the Pilgrim Holiness Church.

Dad was a holiness preacher. He lived it. He loved it. He preached it. He faithfully called people and prayed people into the experience. But he guarded his heart and our home from the critical spirit and overbearing domination of legalism that marked so many of his generation.

The best testimony to his life is the fact that, wherever he went, it was the "sinners" who were most drawn to him.

I want to be like you, Dad. Like Jesus.

Preface

An Open Letter to My Friend, Keith Drury

Dear Keith,

In a couple of years we will hit the twenty-fifth anniversary of your 1995 address to the Christian Holiness Association, "The Holiness Movement Is Dead"

I was browsing in the Holiness Literature section of the John Wesley University library and ran across a book I had never seen before, *Counterpoint: Dialogue with Drury on The Holiness Movement.*

In it, Kenneth Collins, Richard Taylor. Wallace Thornton, Jr. and you were invited to revisit your paper ten years later. It was interesting to listen in to that conversation.

For what it's worth, these are my observations, now approaching twenty-five years later.

1. The more conservative the position, the more mechanical the presentation

Collins stays directly with Wesley and emphasizes "love filling the heart" as the total essence of entire sanctification (too mooshy for the American Holiness Movement). You emphasized the dynamic, progressive and relational aspects of the "experience" (making you the common woman and man's Mildred Wynkoop). Thank you, by the way. Taylor focused on the traditional static stages of the equation (which unfortunately for many became about "me" and "my personal sin management" and never quite got to being about "others", unless in the form of witnessing). Thornton railed away at the apostasy of the "mainline" holiness churches for their pride-driven departure from the external standards once held by all and the abandonment of the "second definite work of grace subsequent to regeneration" terminology.

2. We were a movement sure enough

The American Holiness Movement spanned more than a century. That's
pretty impressive for a movement. We were swept along by the Holy Spirit
and found adherents in any number of Christian traditions. We were
marked by evangelism, holiness, healing, and in time a second-coming
urgency (which Don Dayton properly identifies as the factor that
unfortunately replaced our intentional concern for the poor).

3. We settled down

My observation is that underlying all the observations the four of you made
about the American Holiness Movement is the "human" factor that impacts
all movements: movements cool off, institutionalize and eventually roll to
a stop. By the 1940s and 1950s we had institutionalized into identifiable
local churches, districts, denominations and colleges. Camp meetings were
still going strong, but there were no more prayer bands, and inner city
works were replaced by suburban and rural churches. We became anchored
in those institutions. Anchored people are happy for the winds of the Spirit
to blow across them, but they aren't going anywhere. So, for that reason
and others, the "movement" stalled and died.

4. God is not proud

He worked in, through and among us as a movement as long as we were
fluid and moveable. But he will always move with the movers. So we
watched as he swept the hippies into the Jesus Movement. We watched –
and took up defensive positions – as he swept the Pentecostals and a bunch
of Methodists and even some Baptists into the Charismatic Movement. We
identified with the Evangelical Movement, part of that respectability thing.
We jumped head-first into the Church Growth Movement. In our own
tribe, God used you to lead what is now referred to as the "Youth
Movement", and it produced our church planters, most of our current and
recent District Superintendents, several denominational leaders, and even a
General Superintendent. All the while, whichever movement we
participated in, we brought with us our evolving understanding of holiness,
but we didn't eagerly self-identify in public as holiness people or holiness
churches. Now, other Christian churches and parachurch organizations
have more to say about holiness than we do. God is not proud. He will use
whoever will make themselves available to him to move his purpose

forward. He was willing to use us to bear this message. When we eventually declined to do so, he has found others who would.

5. Is there a movement yet among us?
I hope so. I hope there is a burgeoning Church Planting Movement. I see it stirring. I remember when those of us in the old Evangelism & Church Growth circles used to dream about it. Over four hundred of our crowd (ten percent of the entire conference) recently attended the Exponential East Conference in Orlando. Something seems to be stirring. I hope it's a movement to plant holiness churches.

6.   Did our party pride get the best of us?
Aside from the jealousy that existed among the factions of the American Holiness Movement, there is one factor no one seems to want to talk about. Is it possible the blessing was removed from the Holiness Movement partly because of our prideful exclusion of our Pentecostal siblings? Most American Holiness Movement churches have lived for more than a century pretending that there is no such thing as the Pentecostals (except to demonize them). We do not acknowledge that they too are children of Wesley. Almost all the classic Pentecostals originated from among us. For almost all the classic Pentecostals (except for the 'Jesus Only' crowd), there is only one point of doctrinal difference that divides us. Yet we cannot even seem to summon the grace to invite them in any way to our table. I would think that would probably have a dampening effect on any movement of the Spirit. We don't have to totally agree with them, but shouldn't we find the grace to enthusiastically embrace them?

Anyway, thank you for breathing so much life into our understanding of this wonderful scriptural truth. Thank you for not stopping with your proclamation of the death of the movement, but for going on and writing the wonderful treatment of the doctrine, *Holiness for Ordinary People*. And thank you for having the courage to rattle the nerves of the pretenders twenty-five years ago. I would have loved to have been there when you dropped the bomb!

Thank you, also, for your impact and investment in my life. I am forever grateful. As a young, immature leader, you prophesied Philippians 1:3-6 over me. I have never forgotten that or gotten over it.   – Dan

Introduction

My Grandpa was an engineer on the Chesapeake and Ohio Railway.

I was raised in the little railroad town of Russell, Kentucky. The C&O had built their largest classification yards there. In fact, it was claimed to be the largest in the world at the time, as it said on the masthead of the *Russell Times*, "Home of the Largest Independently Owned Railroad Yards in the Free World".

My grandparents moved there because he was assigned to operate coal trains from Russell to Columbus, Ohio. That is a distance of only about 150 miles, but in that day, with steam engines, it was an all-day haul with numerous stops for coal and water.

His engine was the 2-10-4 T-1 Texas-style engine with two smaller wheels on the leading truck, ten nearly 6' high driver wheels, and four wheels on the trailing truck that bore the weight of the huge Superpower firebox, and cab. The C&O had ninety of those engines and most of them ran out of Russell and up through Ohio to the docks at Toledo. They were restricted to this part of the system because of their weight, being too heavy for the bridges in some other parts of the railroad.

The engine stood seventeen feet high and was over one hundred feet long, with its forty foot long coal and water tender. Together they weighed just under 1 million pounds. That Superpower engine could haul one hundred sixty fully loaded coal cars at seventy miles per hour on flat ground.

Those one hundred sixty coal cars could hold thirteen thousand five hundred tons of coal. That's twenty-seven million pounds of coal! If you took every piece of coal in twenty-seven million pounds of coal and laid them end to end . . . you'd have a long line of coal and you'd be doing that a long time!

It was my Grandpa's job to get that eastern Kentucky and West Virginia coal to Columbus so they could send it to the Great Lakes and all over the Midwest.

The fire in the firebox of the engine was the key to producing the power that could move that massive amount of loaded train cars.

The burning coal in the firebox sent heated air and smoke through a series of long pipes that ran lengthwise through the boiler of the engine, and then expelled the smoke out the smokestack. The water in the boiler was heated to the boiling point by the hot air and smoke, changing it from liquid to steam, which also expanded. The expanding steam was collected in the steam dome at the top of the boiler and as it gathered there it had to go somewhere so it was forced into two pipes that ran to the front of the engine and directed the force of the expanding steam into the two sets of pistons – one on each side – which forced the pistons back in their cylinders in alternating motion.

The pistons were attached to a series of rods that were in turn attached to the drive wheels on the engine frame. As the pistons moved, they moved the drive wheels which moved the engine which pulled the train.

It was a very complicated engineering apparatus that was designed to harness the awesome power of steam and was a wonder to behold as it went into motion with all those moving parts going so fast they became a blur. It was a barely controlled explosion as it clattered down the tracks.

In my childhood, the railroads began to shift to diesel power, resulting in the scrapping of their steam engine fleets. My cousin and I used to sneak over to the Russell yards and climb all over those old engines as they were stored, nose to tail, awaiting the cutting torch. The same engines that used to shake my Grandma's house as they thundered through town, now sat cold and silent, dead.

They looked the same. They still had the same mechanical make-up. They still had the potential for power. Anyone who saw them would say they were steam engines. But they just sat there. Cousin John and I climbed from cab to cab, sat in the same seats the engineers had occupied, yanked on the throttle of each one and pulled the whistle and bell cords, but we went nowhere except in our imaginations.

Why? Because there was no fire in the firebox.

There was no fire in the firebox to heat water that was no longer in the boiler, to create steam that was not there anymore, so we did not move that engine down the track.

The fire in the firebox was the key to the life of that engine.

I want to be very careful what I say next.

I desire to see a rediscovery of our holiness heritage in The Wesleyan Church. I do not desire to imply there is no longer a fire on the altars of our hearts, or in the pulpits of our churches. I do desire to challenge us to fan into flame a hotter fire in that matter of what I believe has become a neglected emphasis in who we are supposed to be – the doctrine of sanctification.

I rejoice in the growth of The Wesleyan Church. I rejoice in the unusual development of the larger churches among us. I rejoice in who our pastors are and how they have a heart for lost people. I rejoice in the breaking down of barriers and the opening of doors that in many places are helping us look a lot more like heaven and a lot less monochrome white. I rejoice in the vitality of our schools. I rejoice in the product of our schools. I rejoice in our gains outside North America. I rejoice in our doctrinal fidelity and our scriptural foundation.

I love The Wesleyan Church.

I love it so much I want to see it become a better and deeper and stronger Wesleyan Church. I want to see it return from its exile in the land of Evangelicalism and see it once again rooted and grounded in the land of our promise and purpose, the land of Holiness.

We have no shortage of evangelical churches in North America. Let the evangelical Methodists, the evangelical Baptists, the evangelical Presbyterians, the evangelical Lutherans and the evangelical Catholics build and support those churches, and let us cheer them on. But who is going to build and populate and support the Holiness churches? We were raised up by God in the midst of the rest of his church to say and live the truth that there is such a thing as a transformed life that is set free from the dominating tyranny of sin and made into the likeness of Christ through the sanctifying power and presence of the Holy Spirit. It is for real. It is for now. It is for us, and all who will embrace and experience this scriptural truth. And we have been assigned the important role in the Church at large, to point the way to this wonderful path of optimistic grace that allows the Church to go deeper and further and higher in our life of faith.

If we do not do this, who will?

Rediscovering our Holiness Heritage: How The Wesleyan Church can get back what we gave away.

PART ONE

HOLINESS IN THE AMERICAN CONTEXT

**How the American Holiness Movement
Said Good-bye to Wesley to
Chase the American Dream**

OVERVIEW FOR PART ONE

The American Holiness Movement was originally
characterized by two dynamics . . .

The first was the bold proclamation that there is more for us than just being saved from sin. John Wesley had famously said, "The least salvation a [person] can have is salvation from sinning." By "sinning" in that statement he meant the deliberate decisions to do something a person should not do, or the decisions to leave undone things a person should do. His American Holiness grandchildren preached that faithfully, and called people to a deeper experience of sanctification with great enthusiasm and great effectiveness. They believed and preached that God could and would "forgive us our sins and purify us from all unrighteousness" – a double cure for a compound problem.

The second was the bold expectation that God wanted to totally reclaim the culture through the power of the Holy Spirit at work in those who would be filled by his presence. The Wesleyan Revival in England led to many great reforms in that society and kept England from experiencing the trauma France had gone through in their revolution. William Booth and the Salvation Army were a direct product and literal embodiment of this bold expectation. The Wesleyan Methodist resistance to slavery, and the Pilgrim Holiness urban storefront churches and downtown rescue missions were direct expressions of that bold expectation.

Sadly, the American Holiness Movement fell into two traps . . .

We began to emphasize certain practices that we felt emulated "holiness" and before long we were measuring people's performance as to how they measured up to our list of expectations. This led in many churches to a dead, performance-based religion instead of a vibrant, love-based relationship with God and our neighbors.

And we preached a brand of personal "heart holiness" that focused on purity and inward cleansing that morphed into a doctrine of self-centered sin management in the life of the believer and neglected the impetus to be released in the power of the Spirit into the broken places in our world. In so doing, we said good-bye to Mr. Wesley and began to pursue a different dream.

CHAPTER ONE

HOLINESS IN THE AMERICAN CONTEXT

How the American Holiness Movement said Good-bye to Wesley to Chase the American Dream

THE PREACHING SHAPED US

Every movement has to be contextualized. The American Holiness Movement was definitely influenced, shaped even, by the North American culture in which it was planted and grew. One reason for that, of course, is that by the time the camp meetings roared into life in the 1800s, and the American Holiness Movement began to develop out of them, the great American experiment in personal freedom and national democracy was into its second century and was peopled by individuals who were products of that culture.

We looked like the Americans we were. We thought like the Americans we were. We acted like the Americans we were. We didn't give it a thought not to, except where we parted ways with the culture over lifestyle and behavior. That culture was one of the greatest formative influences in who we became as a holiness church.

One of the most obvious places it showed up was in the preaching.

Holiness preaching in North America from the start was straight out of the frontier and was "camp meeting" style. Rugged individualism and the American Dream produced holiness preaching that focused on individual growth and effort, and promised purity and power. The "love" that was so central to Wesley's understanding of scriptural holiness got scant mention by American Holiness Movement preachers. It was just not robust and (sorry ladies) manly enough.

When people were called to holiness, they were called to an experience of personal cleansing by fire. And they were called to holiness all the time. The vast majority of preaching was about some form or aspect of the second blessing, the second definite work of grace, sanctification – instantaneous and climactic.

Yes, we were reminded often to love one another, and love God, and love our neighbor, but Wesley's warning that if we seek anything but more love, we miss the mark was nowhere near being central to the typical preaching of the American Holiness Movement.

Power and purity. That was the American way.

Holiness in the American Holiness Movement preaching was all about the personal dimension. Individual. Heart holiness. Something between you and God. It eventually devolved into personal sin management. The promises regarding the work of sanctification in the heart of the believer were almost entirely internally focused. But there was a lot of external behavior that was expected, demanded, and eventually codified to demonstrate the reality and authenticity of that inward work. Externals were seen as the evidence of that inward work.

The further we got from our "poor" roots and experienced the payoff of the American Dream, the more disconnected we became from a central theme that was a focus of the early preaching: the power of the Holy Spirit in our lives sending us out, helping the downtrodden be set free from the things that bound them.

By the mid-twentieth century, virtually the only call to go out was the call for evangelism or missions. It was seldom connected to a concern for the abandoned places and poor people.

It became all about us.

It was almost as if our purpose became "quality control" and our mission became: How can we produce more and better sanctified Christians? Do you get the irony here? We took the distinctive doctrine of "holiness", which is supposed to be about dying to self and enthroning Christ as the unchallenged Lord of our lives in order for us to become a wave of righteousness sweeping away Satan's kingdom . . . and we instead enthroned ourselves while selfishly twisting holiness into being all about "our" purity, "our" power (was "our" pride at the root of that, do you suppose?).

And eventually that's what was preached from the holiness pulpit. "Personal heart holiness" we called it.

In the Pilgrim Holiness preaching I heard in churches, revivals, camp meetings, conferences and college chapels, Wesley was seldom mentioned, but other holiness Methodist preachers were quoted all the time. Especially the ones who made great claims about what the work of sanctification would do in the heart and life of the believer. And we loved to quote each other. The grander the claims, the better.

But Wesley, it seems to me, may have been just too tame or cultured for the Pilgrim Holiness version of the American Holiness Movement. Or maybe too Methodist? Or too high church, formal Anglican?

I'm not sure this neglect of Wesley was as true for the Wesleyan Methodist side of the family. But it was true of the Pilgrim circles I moved in. It was a DNA thing.

Regardless, the sanctified American Dream became the promise we pursued, and even the preaching throughout the entire American Holiness Movement was immersed in it.

Is there rising a generation who has the courage the step over the bones of the American Holiness Movement and go back to Wesley?

Is there a growing understanding that a person's heart should be purified – what Wesley called, "Love filling the heart, expelling sin" – for a purpose beyond itself?

Is there a hunger among us to hear about and experience the kind of personal holiness that presses us out of our comfort and into the fray? That exerts its power in behalf of the poor, the hungry, the thirsty, the neglected, the naked (we have plenty of those folks around), the lost, the imprisoned, the addicted?

Can we preach from a burning heart in a way that catches others' hearts on fire, that sweeps in flames across the landscape and burns the strongholds of Satan to the ground? Can we take that fire outside the four walls of our buildings, maybe? Sometime soon?

The American Dream is an empty illusion. The American Holiness Movement is dead (so our friend had the courage to say).

Is holiness preaching, true to the Bible and true to life, also dead among us?

CHAPTER TWO

HOLINESS IN THE AMERICAN CONTEXT

How the American Holiness Movement said Good-bye to Wesley to Chase the American Dream

OUR GOVERNING PRINCIPLES EMPOWERED US

There would be no King among us.

I was intrigued when I read *American Saint: Francis Asbury and the Methodists*, by John H. Wigger, how Bishop Asbury, by the sheer power of his will, was able to overcome the American independent spirit in his frontier preachers and people, and impose the force of episcopacy upon them.

The early Methodists spread like wildfire in the developing nation, largely through the anointed ministry and sanctified energetic determination of Asbury's circuit riding preachers. He himself rode the circuit from church to church and conference to conference his entire ministry life.

His biggest battle was pushing against the desire of his preachers to "locate", to settle down with their families and pastor people in one place. His determination to push against this cost him many, maybe his best, preachers. But the Bishop pressed on.

In church governance, the American value of democratic representation was ignored. From Asbury on for a great number of decades, only ordained ministers made up the regional conferences and the General Conference of the Methodist Church in North America.

The power, and abuse of power, in the episcopal system was an enormous factor in the 1843 formation of what became the Wesleyan Methodist Church.

In the stormy years leading up to the War Between the States, the southern Methodist bishops were putting pressure on the northern bishops to quieten the ruckus being raised by abolitionist clergy. When they came to their respective conferences in 1842, a number of the trouble-makers found themselves reassigned to remote posts, or given no assignment at all. By Christmastime of that year, the five principal leaders – Orange Scott, Luther Lee, Jotham Horton, LaRoy Sunderland and, on December 26, Lucius Matlack – had withdrawn from the Methodist Episcopal Church, and in the new year formed the Wesleyan Methodist Connection in America. A number of pastors and many of their people, already tightly connected in their opposition to slavery, came out with them to form this new and separate Methodist body. And there would be no Bishop among them.

Two foundational factors developed as a result of their episcopal experience. First, they became the second denomination in North America to provide for lay representation at their conferences. Second, they formed a rigid congregational structure to ensure the power remained with the people. Both of these aspects would have been totally foreign to Wesley, and were direct products of the American culture of personal freedom and independence of expression, with high value placed on representation in the places where decisions are made.

Their Pilgrim Holiness partners-to-be shared their cultural affinity for independence and popular representation, as well as their Methodist theology, but not their Methodist DNA. They were an amalgamation of "come outers" who had left their mainline churches, with a good number of sanctified Quakers thrown in, to follow the deeper path of holiness. They were born out of camp meetings and brush arbor meetings (what we would call church plants) and came together to form independent holiness churches that eventually found each other and formed into a denomination.*

If you listen to the hall talk at a Wesleyan Church General Conference, you will hear an occasional complaint about "creeping Federalism" in the church from someone with Wesleyan Methodist memory, opposing the persistent moving of power to the top and away from the people.

Interestingly, both those sentiments – power with the people and power at the top – are opposite but genuine expressions of the American Dream.

The Pilgrims had no history of episcopal abuse. They formed out of the holiness revival that erupted in the 1800s. As a result, they developed into a pastor-led organization. Still centered in the local church, but not congregational.

Since the merger in 1968, it is not difficult to make the case that The Wesleyan Church has become increasingly pastor-led, with only a few vestiges of the congregational DNA identifiable, although certain former local Wesleyan Methodist churches and at least one district still operate in a very congregational fashion.

When I served as a District Superintendent, I could always tell, even fifty years after the merger, whether I was in a former Wesleyan Methodist church or former Pilgrim Holiness church, simply by the operating philosophy that directed that local church.

The downside of the old Wesleyan Methodist system was its cumbersome demand that every major decision had to come all the way back to the local churches to be ratified. Of course, the crafty among them figured out how to make that work to their advantage resulting in the abuse of control from the bottom. The downside of the old Pilgrim Holiness system was the abuse of control from the top. Ambitious or agenda-driven preachers could figure out how to take advantage of good-hearted people and get their way. Both systems would have been suspicious to John Wesley, a lifelong Anglican who loved order and tradition. He would have immediately seen the encroachment of American democratic ideals into the operation of the church. The poor old fellow would probably have a very difficult time observing all the voting and debating at one of our General Conferences!

Is a democratic-based church government an expression of sin in the church? No. It's an expression of humanness in the church. Every system is a humanly contrived convention that is expected to operate in a broken world full of fallen people. No one system is more "holy" than any other, whether episcopal or congregational or in between. No system is more holy than any other just because it originates out of Catholic tradition, Reformed reason, Anglican order or American ambition. But it sure helps if the "sanctified holy" who are anointed by the Holy Spirit are the ones appointed by us to provide the leadership for us.

Let there be only One King among us!

---

*Regarding how the streams came together to form the Pilgrim Holiness Church, it would be an interesting study to see how these groups in the early years had a real desire to coalesce into a larger group, and then in later years how prevalent church splits and group splits became among them.

CHAPTER THREE

HOLINESS IN THE AMERICAN CONTEXT

How the American Holiness Movement said Good-bye to Wesley to Chase the American Dream

WE SANG A DIFFERENT SONG

When John and Charles Wesley wrote songs about the saving and sanctifying experience (Charles wrote most of them, over six thousand), they wrote from the perspective of God taking the initiative to move toward us in saving and sanctifying grace.

When the American Holiness Movement came along in the next century, deeply entrenched in the Great American Dream, they tended to write songs from the perspective of God waiting on us to initiate a move toward him.

Let me show you what I mean.

Hymn #1 in all Methodist hymnals is Charles Wesley's *magnum opus*, "O For a Thousand Tongues to Sing!" In it he writes that God "breaks the power of cancelled sin and sets the prisoner free." The reference, of course, is to the double application of grace, cancelling our sin debt (our actions and attitudes) in justification and breaking the power of our natural orientation to self and sinfulness (our state) in sanctification. God initiates that whole scenario through prevenient grace, and we respond.

In the opening stanza of "Love Divine! All Loves Excelling", God is the actor, we are the acted upon, as he is the "joy of heav'n to earth come down." He fixes in us his humble dwelling as he visits us with his salvation, entering every trembling heart. God acts upon us, for us, as we receive his mercy and grace. In the second verse, we are promised God's further initiating grace in the form of our "second rest", as he takes away our bent to sinning, setting our hearts at liberty. (This "sanctification" wording aggravated the Baptists, Lutherans and Presbyterians to the point they changed the words in their hymnals.)

In that great hymn of assurance, "Arise, My Soul, Arise!" you might expect that to be us taking action and God responding, but not really. We are arising in response to the fact that, prior to us doing anything, "Before the throne my Surety stands", and as we arise in response each of the redeemed finds "my name is written on his hands."

"And Can It Be?", my personal favorite of the Wesley hymns, shouts the glory of God's active love, incredulous to us, seeking us out and bringing us into full deliverance through our relationship with him. "Long my imprisoned spirit lay, fast bound in sin and nature's night. Thine eye diffused a quick'ning ray. I woke. The dungeon flamed with light. My chains fell off! My heart was free! I rose, went forth and followed Thee! Amazing love, how can it be? That Thou, my God, shouldst die for me!" Again, God initiating the action and doing more than just forgiving us. God leading us into a deeper walk after deliverance. God taking the lead. Us responding.

Contrast that with some of our holiness songs (which by their nature are almost all "experience" based).

"Come Unto Me" promises, "He will sanctify you if you claim his best. In the Holy Spirit he will give you rest." I like that. I've found that to be true. But I also detect that old appeal to the American entrepreneurial spirit. The action of God is in response to the action we take.

"Blessed Assurance" was my Methodist grandmother's favorite song, and really captures the cardinal doctrine of the assurance of sins forgiven and the personal peace which that assurance brings, so highly valued by Wesley. But even that song is influenced by the overconfident American spirit when we proclaim, "Jesus is mine" – not me being his by virtue of his redeeming action toward me.

My other, holiness, hanky-waving grandmother would stand at her seat and sing her testimony, "Standing somewhere in the shadows you'll find Jesus! . . . and you'll know him by the nail prints in his hands." It does a young boy good to witness such a thing. (He's waiting there for you, Danny Gene. Go find him.)

One of the classic American holiness songs is titled, "Satisfied". The chorus says, "Hallelujah! I have found him whom my soul so long has craved. Jesus satisfies my longings. Through his blood I now am saved!" Great song. Great message. But once again you see the orientation of us initially seeking God, not the other way around.

"Once I was bound in sin's galling fetters. Chained like a slave I struggled in vain. But I received a glorious freedom when Jesus broke my fetters in twain", proclaims Nazarene Haldor Lillenas' holiness hymn, "Glorious Freedom", another great rousing song of optimistic grace. It seems to imply our struggle initiates a response from our waiting Savior.

"All to Jesus I Surrender" is a beautiful expression of personal consecration to Christ. "All to him I freely give. I will ever love and trust him, in his presence daily live." Our full consecration is met with entire sanctification in the final words of the fifth stanza, "O the joy of full salvation! Glory, glory to his name." We act in consecration. God responds in sanctification.

Would you be free from the burden of sin? Would you o'er evil a victory win? Would you be free from your passion and pride? Come for a cleansing to Calvary's tide. Would you be whiter, much whiter than snow? Sin-stains are lost in its life-giving flow. There's power in the blood! (It's here for you. Come and get it!)

I love these songs. They are beautiful expressions of the optimistic grace we believe and preach – and used to sing. In spirit, they are a combination of that robust camp meeting "go get it" attitude wrapped in that basic Arminian building block of "the free will".

My point is not that these are bad songs. They are great songs. My point is not that they are theologically inferior songs. They are not. My point is simply that they are a different song than the songs the Wesleys sang. Theirs tended to be more focused on God's actions toward us. The American Holiness Movement songs tended to be more about our actions bringing a response from a waiting God.

There are exceptions, of course.

A couple of traditional holiness songs that I love do show a more Wesley-an orientation in their lyrics.

One of those is, "The Comforter Has Come". The Good News of our pro-active Savior is captured in this verse: "The long, long night is past, the morning breaks at last, and hushed the dreadful wail and fury of the blast, as o'er the golden hills the day advances fast! The Comforter has come!" It brings tears to my eyes and joy to my heart just to read those words.

"Holiness Unto the Lord" is another song that swims against the American Dream tide in American holiness hymnody. It is all about us being "Called unto holiness" by the invitation of God. "Called from the world and its idols to flee. Called from the bondage of sin to be free."

Today we sing a different song than either the Wesley brothers or the American Holiness Movement folks sang. I love our songs today, and the spirit of worship in our churches. They are encouraging, full of praise and based in scripture. And they mention "holy" a lot. And sometimes "holiness" gets mentioned. But it's all about God's holiness. When is the last time you heard any reference to the imparted righteousness of God to us to transform us into the likeness of Christ – with victory for us over sin – in one of our modern songs?

I yearn for a whole wave of songs to sweep across us testifying to the experience of a sanctifying grace that breaks sin's downward pull and sets our hearts to singing with joy. I yearn for the rising generation to experience such a deep conversion of their souls that they can't contain themselves and they have to sing about it. I yearn for a rediscovery of that true holiness that exalts God, gives victory over sin and makes me love everybody!

I yearn for our people to experience it and sing about it again!

CHAPTER FOUR

HOLINESS IN THE AMERICAN CONTEXT

How the American Holiness Movement said Good-bye to Wesley to Chase the American Dream

OUR MEMBERSHIP STRUCTURES BUILT WALLS INSTEAD OF BRIDGES

Among the hallmark values that marked John Wesley's understanding of the ideal Christian life was the belief that behavior was to be taken seriously as an expression of who we are in Christ.

Samuel, his Anglican pastor father, contributed to John's love for order and form in his religious practice, but it was Susanna, his Puritan mother, who instilled in him a love for piety and purity and practicality in the living of the Christlike life. The importance of this to John and his brother and their friends shows up in their formation of and involvement in the Holy Club in their college days and after. They established a methodical system to give direction to their daily decisions and to hold them accountable to each other for the actions and spiritual quality of their lives.

It was religion at its finest.

After Georgia ("I went to America to convert the Indians; but oh, who shall convert me?") and his encounter with the Moravians revealed to him that he needed something more than what he had and awakened a hunger in him for that something more, John experienced the life-changing, heartwarming encounter at Aldersgate which moved him from servanthood to sonship in his relationship with God.

This led, among many other things, to a lifetime commitment to build a robust and effective discipleship process to lay alongside his beloved Anglican Church to bring renewal and vitality to that institution.

The system included societies (neighborhood groups) made up of classes and bands. At the risk of oversimplifying, we could understand the classes to be for instruction in the faith and how to go deeper in a relationship with Christ. The bands were smaller groups designed for serious accountability. The system itself took on a life that even Wesley probably never anticipated. This became the genius of the perpetuation of the Wesleyan movement. His friend and sometime critic George Whitfield testified to this as the two men approached the end of their lives when he lauded Wesley for the way he had been able to preserve his lifetime of ministry influence through this system of discipleship, while referring to his own work, which lacked this systematic approach, as "a rope of sand." (Note that there is no Whitfieldan Church in your town.)

The Methodists in North America were in a much more fluid state than the Methodists in Great Britain at the end of Wesley's life in 1791. They were a system of circuits in a developing society that had little social fabric in many places. But as the population pressed westward and the North American experiment in democracy coalesced into a more structured society, the Methodist system was able to develop and strengthen in the culture. That meant the Methodist churches in North America took on the role of the Methodist "societies" in Great Britain, and the local church membership requirements mirrored the society membership requirements in the old homeland. Over time, the Methodists drifted away from the classes and bands and developed a less strenuous, more casual discipleship structure, replacing it in most churches with the Sunday school and the midweek prayer meeting. The membership structure based on the societies, classes and bands concept stayed intact for a long time, however.

The Wesleyan Methodist Church maintained this membership philosophy at their formation in 1843, all the way to the merger with the Pilgrim Holiness Church to create The Wesleyan Church in 1968. By the time the American Holiness Movement formed into local churches and denominations, they also adopted this membership philosophy in their churches, except for the Church of God (Anderson) which has maintained open local church membership as their standard. In adopting this philosophy, the churches of the American Holiness Movement, of which The Wesleyan Church is one, out-Wesleyed Wesley in two ways.

First, they bought into the self-sufficient "rugged individual" nature of the American culture, uncritically, which resulted in them walking away from Wesley's highly structured discipleship system and leaving a person's spiritual development as a matter of that person's personal business. There was discipleship and there was accountability, but it was nowhere as structured or systematic or strenuous as what Wesley had developed. It was Sunday School and Preaching and Prayer Meeting – but the intimate, regular, methodical examination of a believer by a fellow believer that Wesley established was virtually non-existent.

Second, that they used the requirements for membership in the societies as their requirements for membership in the American Holiness Movement churches, it can be argued, was a significant departure from Wesley.

Wesley was establishing a discipleship movement, not a church. He remained a member of the Church of England his entire life. The Methodist Church as a denomination in Great Britain developed after his death. In America, Asbury and Coke were blasted by him for presuming to consecrate themselves as bishops of what they termed the Methodist Episcopal Church in America. He wasn't about building a "church". He was about building a movement of sanctified holy people to revive and renew the Church. The people he was working with were already, for most of them, baptized members of a church, the Church of England, and he was building a discipleship movement alongside that church.

That Wesley understood it that way can be inferred from the word picture he drew of the Christian life: Repentance is the porch, Justification is the door, Sanctification is the house. A believer enters the faith and fellowship of the Church through the door and lives in fellowship with other believers, all growing in sanctifying grace in fellowship together. Thus Wesley's declaration of this understanding, "The gospel of Christ knows of no religion but social; no holiness but social holiness", does not play well in American Holiness Movement circles, since to us it became all about "personal" holiness. ("Social holiness" in this context does not mean narrowly the intervention of holiness people in social issues, although that is an important part of the understanding, but it means more broadly that we grow in grace in fellowship together and the New Testament knows of no other way of doing it except doing it together.)

The American Holiness Movement, in adopting the model of society membership as the model for local church membership, essentially declared that a person could not bear our name until it was established that he or she was demonstrably living the sanctified life. So how did that work out for us? We made a deliberate decision not to follow the New Testament pattern that seems obvious that "membership" was organic and entry level, included any who were saved and baptized and added to the church, and that relationship then placed those believers on a path of discipleship which, by the power of the Holy Spirit, produced fully sanctified servants of Christ and the kingdom.

We decided, in our American optimism, we could improve on that. Unfortunately, we ended up building walls of protection instead of bridges of invitation.

What we did with membership is understandable, given the sectarian nature of the development of the American Holiness Movement as a group of people coming out from the mainline churches in order to pursue the deeper life with other so committed believers. It is defensible in terms of mission. We took our life in Christ seriously and we did not hesitate to call people to a higher and deeper walk of faith. The sanctified life was the life we desired to live and preach, and we understood this level of commitment was not something everyone would respond to. It is the nature of the flesh to look for fire insurance and be satisfied with that. It is not common for the flesh to allow itself to be crucified with Christ in order to live the more excellent way. Asking people to move in that direction is one thing. Asking them to start there is something entirely different.

In its context it is understandable, and in many ways defensible. But it's not Wesley.

CHAPTER FIVE

HOLINESS IN THE AMERICAN CONTEXT

How the American Holiness Movement said Good-bye to Wesley to Chase the American Dream

OUR WORSHIP INSPIRED US

Worship in most American Holiness Movement churches was very "free church" in its expression, and very non-Anglican. The Church of England, like the people of England, preferred a very orderly, scripted pattern of worship. Not us. It was the camp meetings, out of which the holiness movement was born and grew, that had the greatest influence on how the American Holiness Movement people worshipped.

In John Wesley's experience a century earlier, everyone knew what was going to happen and when it was going to happen in the worship service. That was the orderly English way. It was printed right there in the Book of Worship. Not always so in the American Holiness Movement churches during the nineteenth century and on for over half the twentieth century.

The normal schedule of services involved Sunday school and "Preaching" on Sunday morning, a Sunday evening service, and Prayer Meeting on Wednesday night. As the American Holiness Movement matured, the Sunday school numbers in the local churches were usually higher than the numbers for Preaching. In general, the strength of a local church was measured by the Sunday school attendance. Counting the attendance and reporting it for the morning worship service is a relatively late development in The Wesleyan Church, for instance. People who were not members or who were not professing believers tended to come to Sunday school but not stay for the preaching service.

The Sunday evening service was a preaching service, and for a good part of our history was evangelistic. Believe it or not, there was a day when not-yet believers who would not stay for the Preaching service on Sunday morning would actually show up for the Sunday evening service. Don't ask me why, because in my experience, Sunday night was Sunday morning only not as good.

Prayer Meeting was a smaller weeknight gathering of those who took their faith and their faithfulness seriously. It usually involved opportunity for singing together, sharing personal testimonies and times of praying together focused on prayer requests. In many places the praying was done on your knees at your pew, out loud, and all together -- "the thunder of the saints". It was a beautiful thing to experience.

There was a lot of freedom allowed in the worship services. Personal testimonies on Sunday morning were not unusual, and often sought ("Does anyone have a testimony this morning?"). One of the indicators of the presence and blessing of the Holy Spirit on the service was the report, "People started testifying" or "People started coming to the altar" and "The preacher didn't even get to preach today!"

Fewer hymns than testimony songs and gospel songs were sung in the congregation. We rarely sang a Wesley hymn in my experience.

We sang our songs exuberantly, reflecting the assurance of our salvation and the joy it brings. In places, as the Spirit moved, we sang through a song and sang a verse or chorus again. I was in one service where the pianist, who led the song service in this particular church whether there was a "song leader" or not, led us through four verses of the song, then sang back through the song from the last verse to the first, and then took us back through it from the start one more time! It was glorious.

And there was "special music". While the congregation participated enthusiastically in the congregational singing, there was "special" singing performed by a soloist, duet, trio, quartet, small group or choir. Sunday morning always had at least one special song, and special songs in the evening service were not unusual. That smaller service also served as the place for folks to try out to see if they were ready for Sunday morning.

We were not given an Order of Worship to follow. But we all knew what was happening next. There was no "formality" at all – that was considered unspiritual and seemed too much like human effort intruding on the sacred, but we still had an established pattern, whether it was written on a piece of paper or not. In one church my dad pastored, they took great pride in their informality. In fact, every Sunday the leader would say, "We follow no form or fashion here." Every Sunday. Same words. Same pattern. I'm sure he never caught the irony of that. (They took great pride in their sanctification too, but that's another story.)

The tone of the Sunday morning service in our churches was directly and intentionally challenging, either calling "sinners" to repentance and new life, or "backsliders" to turn back again to their life of faith and faithfulness, or believers to the deeper life of sanctification. Altar calls were not just extended but were expected. In many cases, the pastor's spirituality was measured in direct relation to his consistency and effectiveness in giving an altar call.

In many places it was not unusual for someone to express their joy through exuberant shouting. My holiness grandma was a hankie waving shouter. They shouted, but no one spoke in "tongues". That was not going to be allowed among this crowd. You did not cross that line. You could shout, be slain in the Spirit, even run the aisles (or the backs of the pews!), but no speaking in tongues. Many of the mid-century holiness folks would have believed that "tongues" were of the devil, and many were not shy about saying it.

Every local church was expected to have at least two "Revivals" each year, one in the fall and one in the spring. The revival was essentially the Camp Meeting moved indoors and sponsored by a local church. Early on they were two weeks long, starting on a Sunday morning and going through the next two Sundays. Eventually they were reduced to Thursday through two Sundays (this helped the evangelist by not burning a whole week off as in the three Sunday model). Then Sunday through Sunday came into vogue (again, burning a week between engagements for the poor evangelist). Then shorter times and weekend meetings and finally an occasional special event became the pattern.

The denominational magazines, such as *The Wesleyan Methodist* or *The Pilgrim Holiness Advocate*, carried the "slates", the appointment calendars, of the fulltime and part-time evangelists as well as the evangelistic singers. They were the closest we could allow ourselves to come to Rock Stars – them and the missionaries. People had their favorites and would travel around from church to church and camp to camp to hear them preach. The evangelistic workers traveled by train, some by car towing a trailer, and others by bus. They were rarely afforded nice accommodations in a hotel or motel. They usually were entertained in the parsonage, which did not commonly have a guest room. They paid a high price in sacrificed family time to win the world for Christ and get the won ones entirely sanctified in their meetings.

I remember how impressed I was when I read in *The Advocate*, somewhere around page 38 or 39, that P.O. Carpenter was coming to the Kentucky District Camp at Maysville when I was a boy, or E.C. Swanson was coming for a "Revival at Marion (O.) Second", the church my dad pastored when I was in high school. Unfortunately, the economics eventually caught up with the local churches and full time evangelists and full time evangelistic singers became extinct as guest pastors who were already drawing a salary and could come for a "love offering" took over the preaching duties and local talent did the singing.

Regardless of who was doing the preaching or the singing, the message of repentance from sin for salvation, and surrender for the heart-cleansing experience of sanctification remained the same, and the focus was on the call to individuals to get in right relationship with God.

Do you see the pattern here? In local churches with American Holiness Movement DNA, worship was very much focused on the individual experience, and it was informal reflecting the camp meeting approach. There was little development of the "community" aspect of faith as a theological construct. It was all about the individual's heart relationship with God – personal experience, personal salvation and personal heart purity. Our churches tended to be tight-knit, but there was no intentional discipleship structure similar to Wesley's. And the public services of the church were almost exclusively the delivery system for discipleship.

By the 1930s and later, after the triumph of Second Coming theology among us, neither was there much call from the pulpit in these services for the "compassion for the poor" aspect of holiness which was such a hallmark of the earlier holiness work led by people like Seth C. Rees who established somewhere around a dozen homes for unwed mothers throughout the country, and E.E. Shelhammer who invested his life in Rescue Mission work, and Mary Wessles who took two little orphan boys into her home and eventually established what became Hephzibah Children's Home. Most of the American Holiness Movement people were poor themselves, but they did not demonstrate much care for going into places that were poorer than they were. And they were caught up in not being poor anymore if they could help it. In their personal lives, they were in hot pursuit of the American Dream, and somehow saw advancing from poverty to middle class comforts and security as spiritual blessings. They would not have espoused the prosperity gospel, but they definitely saw their rising personal prosperity as clear evidence of God's blessing on their lives. I doubt many of them ever heard of Wesley's self-imposed financial restrictions, living off the same amount of money annually for decades in order to give himself and all he had to the cause, or of his appeal to his people to "gain all you can and save all you can so you can give all you can."

Two significant points of departure from Wesley in worship were the practice and understanding of the sacraments: communion and baptism, especially communion.

For Wesley communion was a necessary means of grace. For most American Holiness Movement churches it was an add-on ceremony once in a while. For Wesley communion was with real wine and unleavened bread. For us it was grape juice* and whatever bread we had handy, cut into small pieces. For Wesley communion was a sacrament – God in his Real Presence meeting with us in a special way, as this was done in remembrance of Christ. For most American Holiness Movement churches it was more symbolism than sacrament. Wesley's practice of receiving communion at every opportunity, daily if possible, was certainly not practiced by the American Holiness Movement people or churches.

His understanding of the sacramental nature of this means of grace was not shared by people like the Pilgrim Holiness folks who had such strong Quaker influence among them. The Lord's Supper, as they preferred to call it, was shared quarterly, if then, and understood as more symbolic than sacramental. Who had time for such formalities, anyway, when you were busy chasing the devil out of town?

As for baptism, even to this day in The Wesleyan Church, it is difficult to get pastors to take Christ's command regarding baptism seriously. The numbers reported for baptisms lag way behind the numbers reported for persons receiving Christ through local church ministries. Even taking into account those who were baptized as infants, the numbers still do not show a serious commitment to this Christ-ordained sacrament. John Wesley likely would not be able to comprehend that.

In The Wesleyan Church family tree, Wesleyan Methodists may well have been different from most Pilgrims in this regard because they emerged prior to the American Holiness Movement and retained much of their Methodist Episcopal DNA. They tended to be more formal in their worship and more Wesley-an in their awareness than the Pilgrims tended to be. But as they got further removed from Wesley and their Methodist roots, they too took on the same patterns as the other American Holiness Movement churches, except maybe for retaining a more formal approach to worship and more affinity for the sacraments, especially communion.

Moving away from Wesley and the Methodists in worship patterns was not all that bad. The worship among us was enthusiastic, exuberant and full of jubilant praise. When it was at its best, it was Spirit-filled and magnetic. We did ourselves no favors when we walked away from exuberant and jubilant worship like that. We did ourselves a big favor when we finally began to accept in the 1970s the worship the Charismatic Movement brought to the church, full of life and enthusiasm. We would do ourselves a bigger favor, now, if we would begin singing testimony songs again, that rise out of the joyous reality of our sanctified hearts. And we would do ourselves an even bigger favor if we were to lead our people into such a deeper, sanctifying relationship with God that they couldn't help but sing about it.

48

I think John Wesley would agree with that part. "Sing lustily and with good courage. Beware of singing as if you were half dead, or half asleep; but lift up your voice with strength."

Let's get our song back.

---

*In accordance with the rules of order in the Methodist Church and the American Holiness Movement churches, unfermented grape juice was the requirement for the Lord's Supper. In response to this conviction, it was Wesleyan Methodist preacher, pharmacist and medical doctor Thomas Bramwell Welch, of Vineland, New Jersey (by then affiliated with the Methodist Church there), who applied the process of pasteurization to grape juice to keep it from fermenting and thus be usable for local churches for communion. He made some pretty good jelly, too.

CHAPTER SIX

HOLINESS IN THE AMERICAN CONTEXT

How the American Holiness Movement said Good-bye to Wesley to Chase the American Dream

WE TOOK A SHORTER PATH

"Every one, though born of God in an instant, yet undoubtedly grows by slow degrees."

This statement by John Wesley represents his understanding of spiritual growth through the sanctifying work of the Holy Spirit. In context, he goes on to say that God is not bound by time. A day or a month is the same as a thousand to him. He can act according to his will at an instant or over an extended period of time. But the implication is clear: his work is ongoing in our lives. As God works in us, and as we surrender to his work in us, over time we become more and more like Christ and less and less like the person we used to be. It is a process of degrees. And it's never supposed to end as long as we have the capacity to cooperate with him working in us.

The writings of Paul to the churches of his day are almost all about this ongoing process – instruction, correction and direction in growing in the grace and knowledge of our Lord and Savior, Jesus Christ, through the abiding and transforming presence of his Holy Spirit.

There were godly people in North America who were used mightily of God to keep this message alive, primarily through the Methodist Church, although there was significant resistance to it within that denomination. God used Methodist evangelist Phoebe Palmer and her Tuesday Meeting for the Propagation of Holiness to fan the flame of Wesley's understanding of Paul's emphasis on sanctification for a good part of the nineteenth century.

Along with Palmer, other holiness advocates brought their influence into the stream of holiness teaching and preaching.

People like Dwight L. Moody, who experienced an "endowment with power" as the result of the prayers of two Free Methodist women in his congregation, which was a dramatic turning point in his ministry.

People like Charles G. Finney, who adopted the "baptism with the Holy Spirit" terminology of Asa Mahan, after he experienced it himself and became a major force in the Second Great Awakening.

People like English Quaker Hannah Whitall Smith whose *The Christian's Secret of a Happy Life* helped fuel the Keswick Revival in that nation, which profoundly influenced leaders like A.B. Simpson in America.

Although all these influences were not necessarily Wesleyan, they were compatible with Wesley. And beholden to Wesley for his reemphasis of this long neglected scriptural doctrine so central to Paul's teaching.

One place where the developing American Holiness Movement stepped beyond Wesley, though, was in its pursuit of the "shorter way", taught by Palmer and her successors in the movement, especially with its emphasis on a crisis experience. Driven by what might well have been the American preference for immediacy, and later bolstered by holiness scholars and the weight they put on Paul's use of the aorist tense in the Greek language of the New Testament, the expectation and insistence on a "crisis experience", right now, became central to American holiness preaching. The aorist tense is used to communicate a completed action at a specific point in time. The call to sanctification was a call to receive it now, fully, in this moment. A climactic consecration with a clear expectation that God would do, right now, what he has promised to do.

There is a boldness to that which is admirable and can be supported by the experience of many people, but there is also a presumption to that which is unsettling. Instead of a humble approach to receiving grace from God when and how in his ultimate wisdom and all-encompassing love he chooses to dispense it, according to his promise, as we wait in humble faith for him to act, there was it seems an American insistence on rightful claims to scriptural promises now. This tended to cloud the gracious aspect of "sanctifying grace", and tended to put in the shade the progressive, ongoing sanctifying work of God in the life of the believer, for the lifetime of the believer.

Not to mention it tended to put us in control of the process that was supposed to set us free from "us". Not to mention it seemed to be, to many people, not true to the Bible and not true to life. Not to mention it seemed to set up an unwise and unwarranted claim that this was the only way to receive this blessing, given the diversity of personality types who do not all respond to every situation the same way with the same experience. Not to mention, when lesser minds and duller thinkers took to the pulpit, they reduced the Christian life down to two trips to the altar, the first for regeneration and the second for sanctification. Not to mention the tendency of other minds given to mechanical processes who were able to reduce this concept into a neat and tidy formula, not messy like real life.

Our "crisis" theology may have distinguished us, but it did not enrich us. It did make our invitations to receive it burn with urgency. And urgency in matters of spiritual growth is not a bad thing. I'd frankly rather have what we had then – an earnest urgency about our relationship with God and others – than a neglect of the doctrine like we are experiencing now. But I would much rather have a teaching that acknowledges we are a diverse and broken people who live in a diverse and broken world that is not neat and tidy. We need a robust faith that takes us deeper into our messy real life as it allows God to redeem every dark corner of our lives according to who we are and how we are wired. A teaching that acknowledges this experience does start at a given point, it is based on an ongoing obedience and surrender, and it goes on for a lifetime.

Mildred Bangs Wynkoop shook up the American Holiness Movement in the 1970s with this kind of teaching with the publication of her book, *A Theology of Love: The Dynamic of Wesleyanism*. At the risk of oversimplifying, it was an appeal to move away from the formulaic, static, crisis understanding of sanctification to a more dynamic, relational understanding. It was a move back in the direction of Wesley, back in the direction of Wesley's emphasis on love.

And it only makes sense, if you were to place the doctrine in the context of relationships. Take a wedding and a marriage for instance. If couples put as much emphasis and preparation into their marriage as they do their wedding, they experience a much stronger marriage. It's the marriage that really matters. It's the ongoing, set apart, love relationship that will last, grow and enrich them for the rest of their lives that matters.

There are specific starting points in relationships, it's true, but there are more than just two crisis events in any relationship. Relationships are dynamic, not static, and this relationship of holiness needs to be understood in dynamic, not static, concepts.

We need more of that.

Twenty years later, it was Keith W. Drury who shook up the American Holiness Movement in 1995 when he declared to the Christian Holiness Association convention, "The Holiness Movement is Dead." Our friend Keith made it clear in his speech that holiness itself was not dead. But we had ridden the Movement to a stop. A stopped Movement is no longer a movement. It was time to dismount. This horse was dead. He then went on to write the classic book promoting holiness and the holiness message in dynamic, relational terms, *Holiness for Ordinary People*, which brought this message out of the clouds and into the living rooms of a bunch of holiness families. True to the Bible. True to life.

We need more of that.

As I reflect on all that has gone before, there are two things I want to say about this whole matter of how to present the message of holiness to this generation.

First, we owe a profound debt to those who went before us. It is easy to sit where we are today and criticize their approach or their understanding. Approaches and understandings are supposed to change. But the zeal and commitment and depth of spiritual life that characterized our friends who came before us should always be appreciated by us.

We need more of that.

Secondly, we should understand and they should understand that a change in presentation is not a rejection of them or their work. It's a change in time. A change in audience. A change in culture. Even a change resulting from the process of growth in understanding. We need to address this wonderful and dynamic and optimistic truth in our generation in a way that appeals to our shallow, profane world, and ignites a fire of desire in their hearts to know God in his fullness and to find that deep and gratifying relationship with him for which they were created.

We need more of that.

A static understanding of life – lost, saved, sanctified, glorified – is not going to convince or attract many in this post-modern, thinking generation. It just is not authentic and so it is not of interest to them. But a life lived in dynamic relationship with Christ, in day-by-day and moment-by-moment obedience to the Holy Spirit, will convince and attract them because it is authentic. It is the way life was meant to be lived and they recognize it and want it when they see it.

We need more of that.

As we walk the longer path of lifelong growth in grace, in the humility of true holiness, he will increase as we decrease. And he will draw them to himself through a life like that.

We need more of that.

CHAPTER SEVEN

HOLINESS IN THE AMERICAN CONTEXT

How the American Holiness Movement said Good-bye to Wesley to Chase the American Dream

OUR CONVICTIONS SET US APART

Any exposure to the teachings of our spiritual grandfather, John Wesley, reveals the underlying expectation of the Christian to live a careful, modest and humble lifestyle.

Holiness in Wesley's understanding produces a positive, progressive impact in a person's character. This holiness of character in turn becomes the foundation upon which a ministry to a broken world is built, a platform from which it is launched. We are changed inwardly, by the Holy Spirit, and charged to glorify God by acting with a purpose to bring change to the fallen world. 'A charge to keep I have ... To serve the present age'.

For Wesley, personal change on the inside was demonstrated by a corresponding change on the outside. Wesley exhibited a strong set of personal convictions himself in the areas of modesty, being frugal, giving generously, avoiding a prideful bearing, dealing honestly, speaking honestly, living in integrity, submitting to accountability, and dressing plainly.

In order to help others experience growth in grace and character, he created a system of accountability designed to build into them and draw out of them actions and attitudes consistent with the character of Christ. The followers of Wesley took their demeanor seriously.

There is a story of one of them, an over-zealous woman, saying to Wesley, "Thy tie offendeth me," complaining that the strings of his tie were too long, which reflected in her opinion a prideful vanity in his manner of dress. Wesley immediately called for a pair of shears and asked her to cut the tie strings to the length she thought proper. And she did. Snip. Snip. Then Wesley, taking back the shears, said to her, "And now, Madam, thy tongue offendeth me!"

True story or not, it represents Wesley's understanding that the inward orientation of personal conviction is more important than the outward exhibition. It is a matter of the heart that affects and directs the outward action and appearance.

The problem is, the outward expression of holiness convictions can be humanly mimicked without a corresponding inner reality of transformation. A person can manage to operate according to an approved checklist of actions and appearance, and therefore claim "holiness", when in actuality they would just be an old carnal person with a checklist.

That is not to take away from the vast majority of Holiness people who lived a godly, humble, modest life of true holiness marked by a love for God and others. They were the real deal. But they became that way from the inside out, not by the imposition of outward actions and appearances outside in.

The American Holiness Movement fully embraced this understanding, and called for people to demonstrate that they had set themselves apart from "the world" by their outward behavior and appearance. As loquacious as Wesley was about living the Christian life in the context of holiness, I'm pretty sure we outdid him on this.

As this philosophy developed across the decades in the American Holiness Movement, it seems we over-achieved, going way past where Wesley went in terms of giving specific direction to his people as to how they should dress, for instance.

And interestingly, it was the male preachers in the American Holiness Movement who very specifically prescribed for the women how they should look and dress. The men had expectations put upon them as well, but nowhere near as much as the women.

The list for women included things like no make-up, no jewelry, no cutting of the hair, modest dress including sleeves below the elbow, high necklines and long skirts and dresses. No tight clothing. No slacks. No shorts. Hair worn up not down in many holiness circles. And it went on and on.

The principles, again, were modesty, plainness, carefulness, giving no cause for attention or distraction, nothing ostentatious. It was the inner beauty of character that was valued over the doctored up beauty of outward appearance.

The American Holiness Movement never would have admitted this, but it essentially came down to whatever the conservative style of the previous generation, that pretty much became the standard for dress in the current generation. A person could look nice, but not stylish.

Of course, extreme examples can be cited in this over-prescribed effort to make people look "holy". I remember reading a story about the Emmanuel and the Immanuel Holiness Church groups in Colorado, I believe, in a friend's blog. As the Emmanuel Holiness Church originally, a fuss arose among them about the number of eyelets in a woman's shoe. Six was okay, eight was across the line into worldliness. (Nobody was going see them anyway, their skirts were so long!) This caused a split in the group, with those leaving taking on the name, Immanuel Holiness Church. Really. The Emmanuels and the Immanuels. I wish that was apocryphal, but unfortunately, it happened.

The list of what you could do and what you couldn't do grew out of personal convictions commonly shared among the group.

No smoking or chewing or dipping tobacco products. This extended to no working in the tobacco industry, no raising tobacco, no selling it, and even some extended the prohibition to working in a grocery store that sold the products.

There was no use of beverage alcohol allowed in any form. And the same kind of prohibitions extended to tobacco were extended to alcohol as well.

Gambling was prohibited. Also prohibited was participation in raffles and lotteries.

The denominational schools embraced and enforced "the list", sometimes more consistently than the local churches the students came from. In college, we could play Rook (a thinly disguised version of spades) but "face cards" were not allowed.

Television was heavily frowned upon when it first appeared. This was an extension of the prohibition of attending movies. Now they were bringing movies into the living room.

Dancing was not allowed.

When I was a teenager at the Eastern Ohio Campgrounds in Coshocton, I had a woman give me a tract on the evils of chewing gum. (It tricked your digestive system into thinking it was going to receive nourishment and that was a moral sin against your body, as I remember.)

We were serious about it.

Wedding bands and engagement rings were not allowed, nor was any other form of jewelry. Earrings ("ear bobs") were off limits.

We were very careful with our language. There would be no profanity, cursing, obscene talk, vulgarities, blasphemy or crudeness escaping our lips. "Minced oaths" like darn or dang or heck or shoot or daggone it or holy cow were not uttered either. As our two year old son told his godly grandmother (yes, that one) when she let one slip, "Mawmaws don't say shoot!"

Not much was said about over-eating, though. That's probably because fat preachers were writing the rules.

"Mixed bathing" was not allowed. In North Carolina, the godly did not go to the beach. We went to the coast.

We even had certain cars we could drive. Chevrolets and Fords were our most common choice. Oldsmobiles and Pontiacs were acceptable. Plymouths, Dodges and a certain level of Chrysler were okay. Ramblers were okay. Buicks were pushing the limit. And no holiness person dared risk his standing by driving a Cadillac.

We were serious about it.

J. Percy Trueblood was a well-known evangelist in the Wesleyan Methodist Church in the early to mid-1900s. He was raised in the rural community of Bagley Swamp in the northeastern corner of North Carolina. He nearly lost his credibility among those folks early in his ministry when a conservative Pilgrim saw him carrying a carton of Coca-Colas into his house. Soft drinks were on the forbidden list for many holiness people, not because of the content, but because they came in glass bottles, in cartons, with press-on metal caps – just like beer.

Another Bagley Swamp man, an ultra-conservative fellow by the name of Mr. Antley, said to his friend, "As far as I know, only two of us from this community are going to heaven, and I'm beginning to be concerned about you!" He went to Elizabeth City to attend a tent meeting where independent Baptist radio preacher Oliver B. Greene was speaking. Mr. Antley was on the front row every night, to help the preacher preach. One night, Greene said, "Some of you people will waste a nickel on a Coca-Cola!", to which Mr. Antley responded in full voice, "Preach it, Brother! Preach it!" Then Greene finished his sentence by saying, "When you could get a Pepsi for the same money!" (Cokes were six ounces, Pepsis were twelve.) Mr. Antley said later, "He set me up. He just set me up."

Back in the day, two young men from the First Pilgrim Holiness Church in High Point nearly got "churched" for going to a University of North Carolina Tar Heels basketball game. Their pastor, J. Adrian Grout, took up for them challenging the local board to tell him where they could find two finer young men than Bill Winslow or Jack Farlow.

We were serious about it.

Many of these personal convictions remained unwritten expectations, but the others were codified into Membership Standards in the American Holiness Movement churches. They were listed in the official rule books and only a vote of the General Conference could change them.

The American Holiness Movement churches went to great effort to protect the list.

In The Wesleyan Church it is ensconced in the Constitution, not in the Statutory Law. It takes a two-thirds vote of General Conference and a two-thirds aggregate vote of the District Conferences to change any item on that list. According to Wesleyan historian Bob Black, we have Conference President of the Wesleyan Methodist Church Roy S. Nicholson to thank for this, but not for the reasons you are thinking. For most today, the issue is liberalizing the list and protecting the list from being liberalized. In Nicholson's Day, he strategically made this move to protect the list from being taken over by the harsh agenda of the austere, ultra-conservative wing of the Church.

The Bottom Line is this:

The list is a human list with divine input through scripture and the leadership of the Holy Spirit, but it is always flawed. It often went too far, and it always fell short. It is never the ultimate authority. Only God through inspired scripture holds that place for us. Then we bring our collective wisdom, our good and bad experiences, and our common knowledge to it.

There were seasons where the list got twisted from being a reflection of the heart to being thought of as the way to produce heart holiness by living slavishly by the list. Changed from being "this is what holiness looks like" to "this is what holiness is". That is legalism. That is human effort. That is not scriptural holiness.

The American Holiness Movement lists were remarkably similar from denomination to denomination. And changes to the lists by one group tended to cause two reactions. When changes were made, other groups would adopt the changes as well (for a long time it was usually the Church of the Nazarene who would make the change first and the other groups would follow). Invariably, the other reaction would be that the changes were intolerable to some in the group and they would leave and join other likeminded folks or start their own group. Then they would throw verbal rocks at the "compromisers" for changing the list.

We were serious about this.

When you over-identify, too highly revere or over-emphasize the list, it becomes unchangeable. Then it takes over the mission. Then it becomes a battleground. Then the group splits apart over it. Too often this happened in our churches.

When I was a District Superintendent, I wanted to build bridges to other holiness groups. I attended an inter-church holiness gathering locally. I've been around a long time so I knew a good number of the people who were there, and I knew which Wesleyan church they originated from. Some were two or three churches removed from their original church. There were probably twelve to fifteen conservative holiness churches represented. And I knew the history of many of them, how they had formed from splits of splits. And I knew the role contention over the list had played in our own sad story as well. Tension that led to fussing that led to a split.

All over "The List".

Our convictions have set us apart over the years. They have also torn us apart. We were serious about it – too serious sometimes.

CHAPTER EIGHT

HOLINESS IN THE AMERICAN CONTEXT

How the American Holiness Movement said Good-bye to Wesley to Chase the American Dream

A VERY DISTURBING QUESTION:
WHY DID THE EARLY WESLEYAN METHODISTS
NOT HAVE ANY BLACK FRIENDS?

There is a disturbing, potentially offensive, easily misunderstood but necessary question I feel I must ask. It pertains more to the Wesleyan Methodist Church specifically but still relates to the larger American Holiness Movement context, as well.

The question is this:
Why did the early Wesleyan Methodists not have any black friends?

John Wesley used his influence on both sides of the pond to bring about the end of human slavery. His tract on "Thoughts upon Slavery" is excoriating for anyone who held that this atrocious practice was in any way acceptable for any human being to experience or condone, let alone support.

The last letter he wrote before his death was to William Wilberforce, a member of Parliament and convert of Wesley's, encouraging him to continue his valiant effort to eradicate human slavery from the British Empire, and praying that the effort would even bring about, by God's great power, the end of the American slavery institution, "the vilest that ever saw the sun."

What someone gives his last breath to is probably pretty important to that person.

Unfortunately, this vile evil would split his American people at least five ways – into the Methodist Episcopal Church-North, the Methodist Episcopal Church-South, the Methodist Protestant Church, the Free Methodist Church, and our own Wesleyan Methodist Church. That's not even to mention the Baptists and the Presbyterians who also split over this issue. And the nation itself, which entered into the bloodiest war of our history – a war fought by some for the freedom to enslave others.

The Wesleyan Methodists were courageous, unintimidated and extremely effective in their opposition. They were no joke. They were staunch abolitionists. Abraham Lincoln was no friend of theirs. He was too accommodating. They wanted an immediate cessation of slavery regardless of the economic or political consequences.

They were heroes for the cause.

To criticize them is kind of like criticizing Simon Peter for wavering in his faith and starting to sink in the waves. Who else got out of the boat? Who else could tell his grandkids, "I walked on water!"? So what criticism there is here is offered with a sensitive spirit.

There is a warning to us from our ancestor heroes. Be careful about falling in love with a cause or issue or idea, and forgetting to fall in love with the people.

After the War Between the States settled the matter of slavery as a moral, political and economic issue in the United States, our history indicates we turned our attention to other matters.

In conversation with Wesleyan scholar Anthony Casey, I became aware of the following. Adam Crooks is one of my heroes, but like all heroes, he was a man of his time. This is his statement in *The American Wesleyan* (the denomination's weekly periodical and successor to *The True Wesleyan* begun by Orange Scott), February 6, 1867 edition, published less than two years after the conclusion of the War Between the States:

> But the chief aim of *The American Wesleyan* shall be to promote the GREAT WORK OF SALVATION in all its stages . . . . Under God, having to some degree been influential in securing the

physical liberty of the oppressed poor of the land, so shall it earnestly labor in co-operative effort with Father, Son, and Holy Ghost, for the higher spiritual liberty of all oppressed by sin and the Devil. Unquestionably, this is the Master want of the world and the Church in the present age.

In other words, we fixed this slavery problem and now we are moving on.

As a result of moving on to what the Fifteenth Quadrennial Session of the General Conference of the Wesleyan Methodist Connection of America in 1899 termed "the grander, nobler work" of promoting heart holiness – "spiritualizing men and exalting the Church of our Lord Jesus Christ" they called it – as opposed to what the church had been doing in its formative years, we focused on a new mission, apparently assuming there was no more to be done in this former arena. We did not integrate newly freed slaves into our churches in the days after the War. Any former slaves who did affiliate with us, we sequestered into a segregated churches in a segregated District, the South Ohio District (defined by ethnicity, not geography), allowing them full access into our denominational activities, but we did not welcome them into our lives, to our tables or into our living rooms.

This came up to bite us big time a hundred years later, during the civil rights era of the 1950s and 1960s. When the calls for human rights began to rise, the later iteration of the Wesleyan Methodist Church, and her Pilgrim Holiness cousins, were silent. When we did speak, it was to criticize and label the movement as wrong, led by trouble makers who had no respect for authority. We were scandalized. We understood the issues, from a distance – a safe distance – but we disapproved of the way they were doing things. Did any of us happen to ask ourselves how the oppressed, disenfranchised, poor, unrepresented, and disempowered are supposed to "do it the right way"?

Hang on, because this is going to sting big time. We hold in highest esteem the Revolutionary War citizen fighters who took up arms and killed their fellow British citizens in order to achieve their freedom. But almost 200 years later, these people sat peacefully at lunch counters, rode busses that were set on fire, marched across bridges arm in arm, walked through blasts of fire hoses, were mauled by ferocious dogs sicced on them by police officers, were beaten and jailed illegally, despised and spat upon and lynched, their children burned alive in their churches, and were shot in the head to lay dying on a motel balcony in Memphis, Tennessee. To gain their freedom.

Why were we silent? Because we did not know any of these people. We had not cultivated a relationship with them or their ancestors across the decades. We were a white, insulated American church living the American dream. And they were nameless, faceless objects of our neglect.

Lord have mercy on us.

To illustrate this shortcoming, Anthony Casey shared an account of a conversation with then retired General Superintendent Virgil A. Mitchell, recorded on video by Matthew Tietje. Dr. Mitchell told of being surprised decades later when someone mentioned that in the 1968 Merging General Conference of the Wesleyan Methodist Church and the Pilgrim Holiness Church to form The Wesleyan Church, no official statement of any kind had been issued regarding the civil rights unrest going on in the nation. Martin Luther King had been martyred in Memphis on April 4, and the Merging General Conference convened in Anderson, Indiana on June 26. Dr. Mitchell felt that surely could not be so, but after a thorough search of the written proceedings it turned out to be all too true. Not a word.

Lord help us.

For years I had prayed for the Lord to forgive us in North Carolina for the bridges we had burned in this area, and for some way to rebuild those relationships. We had always been among the leaders in the denomination in Hispanic ministry. We were able to attract some Caribbean folks. But we just could not break through barriers we had built with the North American black population.

Little did I know that the answer to my prayers was sitting across the dinner table from me.

The Lord used our homegrown prophet, our youngest son, Josh, to start conversations among our pastors we had not allowed ourselves to have.

In a gentle but persistent way, while living what he was saying, Josh opened doors and minds by the help of the Holy Spirit. Now it is more the exception than the rule for our local churches to be all white, as we have seen a beautiful transformation begin to take place. Our ethnic friends are finding their way into our fellowship and they are being met with open arms and hugs around the neck.

And this is the story across the Wesleyan denomination. People like Santes Beatty and Troy Evans, Kim Gladden and Kyle Ray, Paul Tillman and my friend Sidney Wheatley are working diligently to help us look more like heaven by the day. In fact, we think little of the novelty of it anymore. It is who we have become. Thank God!

Lord, continue to bring enriching color to our church family. And help it increasingly to be in The Wesleyan Church as it is in heaven.

CHAPTER NINE

HOLINESS IN THE AMERICAN CONTEXT

How the American Holiness Movement said Good-bye to Wesley to Chase the American Dream

A SECOND VERY DISTURBING QUESTION:
WHY DID THE EARLY PILGRIMS NOT HAVE
ANY PENTECOSTAL FRIENDS?

There is a second disturbing, potentially offensive, easily misunderstood but necessary question I feel I must ask. It pertains mostly to the Pilgrim Holiness side of the family, because of their name and their American Holiness Movement DNA. The essence of the question definitely relates to the larger American Holiness Movement context, as well.

The question is this:
Why did the early Pilgrims not have any Pentecostal friends?

The American Holiness Movement enjoyed a thriving life up through the end of the nineteenth century. Moving into the twentieth century there were some interesting developments in the North American religious atmosphere.

The Adventist emphasis on the immediate return of Christ was stirring people up. The Christian cults were gaining in strength. The American Holiness Movement was rapidly forming into local churches and then denominations.

And somebody started speaking in tongues on Azusa Street.

Up until the Azusa Street Revival in Los Angeles, the term "Pentecostal" belonged to the American Holiness Movement and some Methodist groups. It was used interchangeably with terms such as "Apostolic" and "Holiness".

The Church of the Nazarene was the Pentecostal Church of the Nazarene. Martin Wells Knapp, co-founder of the Pilgrim Holiness Church, led a group called the International Apostolic Holiness Union and Prayer League, and wrote *Lightning Bolts from Pentecostal Skies.* Asbury College's Henry Clay Morrison, renowned Methodist evangelist and educator, later founder of Asbury Theological Seminary, published a periodical called the *Pentecostal Herald.*

After Azusa, however, the terms "Pentecostal" and "Apostolic" pretty much transferred to the groups who advocated speaking in tongues as a sign of the filling of the Holy Spirit, and the "Holiness" churches were from that time forward identifying themselves as not "Pentecostal" or "Apostolic" ("Jesus Only" non-Trinitarian).

Bad blood developed between the Pentecostal groups and the Holiness groups. Mostly, the differences were theological centering on the novel idea of speaking in tongues and adding a third work of grace beyond regeneration and sanctification. The Pentecostals were confident they had recovered a New Testament teaching completely neglected in the Church until this latter day, and now, in a pouring out of God's Spirit upon his people in preparation for the impending return of Jesus, they were experiencing what the Church should have been experiencing all along.

The traditional holiness folks did not believe a word of it. In fact, they pretty much condemned it as false teaching, many even attributing it to the deceit of the Devil. It was "wild fire".

One of the driving issues was the competition for adherents, and the taking over of Holiness churches by Pentecostal preachers and people. The Holiness leaders watched the tongues issue split their churches and divide their people. The early 1900s were years of sharp conflict as the two groups drew territorial lines and faced each other down.

A wide divide developed and any fellowship or cooperative effort between the groups was extremely rare. There is no enmity quite like the enmity that develops within a family.

Where I grew up, in northeastern Kentucky, a "holiness" church was a Wesleyan-oriented church with no connection whatsoever to any Pentecostal church. Ever. When I came to North Carolina in the late 1960s to attend college, I joined the college choir. We toured the Pilgrim Holiness churches in the North Carolina District each spring. I was puzzled my first time around when I saw the church signs. Most of them read, "Pilgrim Church". I thought we were Pilgrim Holiness. What happened? I learned that The International Pentecostal Holiness Church was founded and headquartered in North Carolina. And they were everywhere. The Pilgrim churches got tired of the confusion and dropped "Holiness" out of their names. I guess they would rather be confused with the Congregationalists – not too many New Englanders down here – than the Pentecostals.

The fact that many of the original Pentecostal Holiness churches had started out as Pilgrim Holiness churches didn't help matters much.

The divide never bothered me, really. I was with us. They were with them. Until I had a conversation with the pastor of the Calvary Pentecostal Holiness Church just around the corner and up the road from the Bagley Swamp Wesleyan Church. He was a gentle, godly man. He broke my heart, though, the day he asked me, "Dan, when will you Wesleyans acknowledge that we are children of Wesley, too? We feel like the unwanted step-child not welcome at the table."

All my anti-Pentecostal arguments fell in a heap on the ground.

What is the world is wrong with us? The classic Pentecostals differ from us on one point of doctrine. One point. Can we not have fellowship with these people? Can we not sit down and talk? Can we not find ways to work together? Even though they vastly outnumber us now, we own the table. If The Wesleyan Church somehow were to find the grace to invite our Pentecostal brothers and sisters back to our table, it would shake up the American Church, heal many deep wounds on both sides, and make God smile. Somehow I believe our common Grandfather Wesley might even smile. If he could say to a Roman Catholic, "If your heart is as my heart, here is my hand", then surely we can be Wesleyan enough to love another Wesleyan.

CHAPTER TEN

HOLINESS IN THE AMERICAN CONTEXT

How the American Holiness Movement said Good-bye to Wesley to Chase the American Dream

THE SECOND HALF OF THE GOSPEL

In 2011, Christian researcher George Barna reported the results of a poll conducted over the span of six years with fifteen thousand people in North America, regarding the depth of commitment to their Christian life and faith across the spectrum from Unaware of Sin to Profoundly in Love with God and People, in North America.

Barna identified "ten transformational stops" in a person's spiritual growth and assessed the responses of those polled. The findings are broken down in this way:

Unaware of sin	1%
Indifferent to sin	16%
Worried about sin	39%
Forgiven from sin	9%
Forgiven and active in church	24%
	89%

Holy discontent	6%
Broken by God	3%
Surrender and submission	1%
Profound love for God	.5%
Profound love for people	.5%
	11%

Methodist thinker and leader J.D. Walt, director of *seedbed*, the publishing and conferencing arm of Asbury Theological Seminary, took Barna's report and issued a challenge to the holiness sector of the Christian church in America, to recover our voice and begin speaking again about "The Second Half of the Gospel".

He asks what is the question that matters the most now? And what does God want his people to become? And will we be almost Christian or altogether Christian?

The first half of the gospel is represented by John 3:16,

> "For God so loved the world that he gave his one and only Son, that whoever believes in him shall not perish but have eternal life."

Walt says this verse is clearly the banner and battle cry for that initial introduction to the redeeming grace of God that moves us from our kingdom into his, by confession, repentance and baptism.

The second half of the gospel is represented by 1 John 3:16,

> "This is how we know what love is: Jesus Christ laid down his life for us. And we ought to lay down our lives for our brothers and sisters."

Why is this the banner and battle cry for the second half of the gospel? It represents us abandoning ourselves to the ongoing process of giving ourselves over completely to Christ in love for the sake of others. It clearly and simply and profoundly defines for us what God means by "love".

Nothing is more beautiful or admirable or praiseworthy than people laying down their preferences, claims and rights, their agendas, interests, needs and desires, for the very best interest of other people. Because this is selfless and so like God, we dare to call it "holy love".

In response, he calls for a revolution of sanctification, a renaissance of scriptural holiness among us. He summarizes the words of Count Nicholas Ludwig von Zinzendorf, the Eighteenth Century leader of the Moravian community of Herrhut and a person of great influence in the spiritual development of John Wesley, who said that many people will follow the

Lord half way, but will not go the other half. They will willingly give up possessions and property and wealth, but it touches them too deeply to disown themselves.

That's what the whole gospel is about. It is a whole gospel of the whole truth of scripture for the whole world impacting the whole person.

The rest of the gospel, our friend J.D. says, is the best of the gospel.

There are several issues that come to light from Barna's research, but the most alarming to our faith tradition is the virtual poverty of faith in the second half of the statistics. Only 11% of professing Christians, if the statistics are accurate, fall within the categories that would identify as moving beyond forgiveness and regeneration, into the areas of sanctification.

It is my conviction that the statistics are so dismal because we walked away from our calling and have neglected the "Grand Depositum" handed off to us from Jesus and Paul through Wesley. We have stopped talking about sanctification as a concept. We have stopped preaching sanctification from our pulpits. We have fallen into preaching a "self-help" gospel that could be found in any number of pop psychology texts and chicken soup books more readily than it can be found in the sacred book. We have stopped calling our people to a life of sanctification.

As an evangelical church, we now live in the first half of the gospel. I rejoice in the evangelistic fervor I find in The Wesleyan Church. I do not in any way desire to demean the wonderful miracle of salvation through repentance and faith it Christ. Our churches are growing. Our outreach is increasing. We are among those who are desperately working to close the ever increasing Gospel Gap. We find favor in the Lord's sight for our insistence on calling people out of darkness and into his glorious light.

But if I read the book correctly, there is more. That "more" is not just a call for a certain grade of disciple to move into an elite status reserved for the few that find it. That "more" is the gracious provision of an indwelling Presence to remake us into his image and give us freedom from the domination of sin. It is the Christian's inheritance, the abundant life promised by Jesus, the deeper life of the normal follower of Christ. It is the call to experience a holy discontent with where we find ourselves in our relationship with God, which leads to us being mercifully broken by God until we respond in a surrender and submission to his deeper work in us that produces in us a profound love for God and a profound love for people.

I still use an iPhone 5. I know. Ancient. But when it is fully connected to that 4G network, it just hums along happy as can be. Each year, around my birthday (August 14 if you want to send a card), our dear friends Steve and Debbie give us a week at their log cabin in the mountains of western North Carolina. It is remote and relaxing. You can see the Blue Ridge Parkway across the valley at Phillips Gap from my favorite rocking chair in the shade on the back porch.

Did I mention there's no cell service inside the house? You can get maybe one bar outside if you stand in the right place in the right corner of the back porch. Maybe. My little smartphone wears itself out searching for service. The battery drains in no time. It is not a happy camper.

The purpose of that cellphone is not just to be in constant connection with the signal. The purpose of the cellphone is to use that connection to connect with other people. A connected cellphone is nice but has no purpose. A communicating cellphone is the only reason for a cellphone to exist.

That is a pretty good parallel to our spiritual life. We are designed to live in close contact to the source that gives us purpose. The closer we draw to him, the stronger we are spiritually. When we drift away from him, or we allow things to come between us and him, the signal drops, the striving begins, the frustration builds, and life descends into being all about us. Old patterns tend to try to take hold again. This can tend to be life when it is lived only in the first half of the gospel.

Life represented by the second half of the gospel, the sanctified life, is really simple to understand. It is the life lived in constant connection with the source of our purpose, our Heavenly Father, through an ongoing and uninhibited faith relationship with Christ our Savior, by the indwelling power source the Holy Spirit, who so fills us with the character of our Heavenly Father – godly love – that we find ourselves growing in profound love for God and others.

When you find the signal waning, move closer to your connection to the God who loves you, and then communicate his love to those around you.

Our friend J.D. says the rest of the gospel is the best of the gospel. I'm with J.D. If you have never experienced this, when you discover the reality and beauty and fulfillment of life in the second half of the gospel, you'll understand why.

Then you can be like the fifteenth century explorers whose coins were imprinted with the message there was "No Mas" ("No More") past the Straits of Gibraltar, but who came back with great stories of a whole new world out there. You can be part of that new brand of holiness pioneers to search out this fabled new world of the second half of the gospel, where giants used to dwell, and come back and tell us true tales of the wonders and mysteries you have discovered there. For you, the "best" is yet to come.

CHAPTER ELEVEN

HOLINESS IN THE AMERICAN CONTEXT

How the American Holiness Movement said Good-bye to Wesley to Chase the American Dream

THE SECOND HALF OF THE SECOND HALF OF THE GOSPEL

We need to understand how we and the rest of the American Holiness Movement kept losing the game in the fourth quarter.

This is another of our points of departure from Wesley. From the beginning, holiness people were involved in interfering with the world and its downward pull, especially in the lives of the poor and marginalized, those most vulnerable. When proper gentleman and insolated clergyman John Wesley began that "vile" (his word) practice of field preaching, he drew large crowds. It was not unusual for them to number in the thousands. And who made up the crowds? The common people, especially the poor.

As a result, the Wesleys began to intervene in behalf of their "Methodists" such as the impoverished and mistreated coal miners of Somerset. That led to intervention in matters of child labor, illiteracy, health issues, and the like. This movement gave birth to Methodist preacher William Booth's Salvation Army. It put hands in the back of folks like William Wilberforce, pushing him to use his position and influence in Parliament to bring down the slave trade in the British Empire.

Among the Methodists in North America, a group arose in opposition to American slavery. They agitated with such fury that the Southern bishops put pressure on the Northern bishops not to appoint these pastors to churches. And you know the rest of the story – the birth of the Wesleyan Methodist Church.

After the Civil War resolved the issue of human slavery in America, the group continued to use its *True Wesleyan* voice to thunder away at social vices such as gambling, alcohol consumption and prostitution. And they advocated for the rights of women, with the first Women's Rights Convention being held in the Wesleyan Methodist Church in Seneca Falls, New York. The first woman ordained in North America asked Luther Lee to preach her ordination sermon. This group found its way into the American Holiness Movement through a common love for the proclamation of sanctification and involvement in independent holiness camp meetings. Another group, the other half of The Wesleyan Church, began to develop in the late 1800s as part of the American Holiness Movement. They too were marked by their "shake the devil's kingdom to the ground" activism. They went where respectable people would not go. They established storefront missions in urban centers. They fed, clothed and sheltered the poor. They rescued women from prostitution and provided shelter for unwed mothers. They closed bars by getting everyone in the place saved. And they ordained women. The first two people ordained in the Pilgrim Holiness Church were a man and wife. (So at least at one point in our history, one half the ministers ordained in the Pilgrim Holiness Church were women.)

So what happened? Two things happened that are directly related to each other, one growing out of the other. The Adventist theologies that made people gather on hilltops in the late 1800s, awaiting the immediate return of Christ, were sanitized and sanctified by conservative Christians in the early 1900s and this teaching swept through the ranks, including taking the American Holiness Movement by storm. Don Dayton, in his book, *Discovering an Evangelical Heritage*, observed that a seismic shift took place in conservative churches, and evangelism suddenly became the only thing to do, in light of the possible immediate Return of Christ. This fascination with the Second Coming, and the corresponding fervor for evangelism, fueled the rise of the Evangelical Movement, and the American Holiness Movement got swept right along with it. Elaborate theories emerged about pre-millennial or post-millennial, pre-tribulation or post-tribulation, or – maybe – mid-tribulation return theories, all using the same scripture passages, but arranging them in different sequences. Any evangelist worth his salt had a fifteen-foot-long banner illustrating his perception of coming events.

The second development came from the respectability the Evangelical Movement enjoyed in the Christian culture of North America as it grew, and the American Holiness Movement coincidentally shared in that. Pursuing the American Dream, over time we moved out of the lower-class areas and into the safety of the suburbs. We got the respectability we so wanted. (Ironically, we were now "respected" by groups we preached against.) We settled into our comfortable churches and focused on our personal sin management, which we called sanctification, and heard little about or from those crying in the night. Along with our close cousins in the American Holiness Movement, we abandoned our heritage of incarnational discipleship. We turned discipleship into learning facts in a classroom – facts that should have transformed us and compelled us to respond to the needs within our reach, but they didn't anymore. They just piled up in our brains and sat there, like we did.

Sadly, the only thing we told our people to do outside the four walls of the church was to live a holy life. That would lead to "witnessing" which was our replacement for the incarnational ministries that used to be one of our defining marks. But since we didn't know the urban poor anymore, we were no longer moved with compassion for them.

We kept losing the game because we kept failing to show up for the fourth quarter. We got our people into the Word. We helped them with their spiritual disciplines. We bound them together into the community of the Spirit-filled. But we seldom took them outside the walls. "Personal holiness" owned the pulpit. How ironic. The signature work of God in the life of the maturing believer that is designed to dethrone us, enthrone Christ, and compel us to move with power and purity into the darkness, that work we call "sanctification" – we took it and twisted it and made it all about ourselves. Personal holiness.

So what needs to happen?

There is hope. There is a generation rising that understands that we gather for worship, inspiration, encouragement, instruction and care, but the work is outside the walls. So they headed out to Grand Rapids and New York City and Boston and Los Angeles and Portland and Chapel Hill and Indianapolis and Detroit and Chicago and the list goes on.

They are embedded in their communities. They are doing what their great-grandparents did. They are reconciling and healing and empowering and beating back the darkness and obeying the call. They are close enough to the hurting to know their names and what their needs are. They are close enough to hear the cries and brave enough to do something about it. They are winning the game in the fourth quarter!

Now let's get up and go with them. And let's pray for them, and for us, that in winning the game in the fourth quarter we don't lose the game in the third quarter by not understanding that human effort alone will not get this done. Only the sanctifying work of the Holy Spirit that brings purity and power will enable us to "break the power of cancelled sin and set the prisoners free"!

Let's not lose the game in the third quarter by thinking we make eternal changes in a person's life when we are only making temporal or circumstantial changes. It's the whole gospel for the whole person, or it falls short. Let's clothe our friend in warm clothing as we clothe our friend in the righteousness of Christ.

PART TWO

HOLINESS ECLIPSED

**How The Wesleyan Church
Sold Its Holiness Birthright in Order to
Become an Evangelical Church**

"By salvation, I mean, not barely (according to the vulgar notion) deliverance from hell, or going to heaven; but a present deliverance from sin, a restoration of the soul to its primitive health, its original purity; a recovery of the divine nature; the renewal of our souls after the image of God in righteousness and true holiness, in justice, mercy and truth."

John Wesley

CHAPTER TWELVE

HOLINESS ECLIPSED

How The Wesleyan Church sold its Holiness birthright in order to become an Evangelical Church

WHERE DID THE EVANGELICAL MOVEMENT GO?

The North American version of the Evangelical Movement emerged in the mid-twentieth century as a more moderate, middle way between the liberalism born out of the German theological influences of the late 1800s and early 1900s that swept through the seminaries of the mainline churches on one side, and the reactionary Fundamentalist Movement on the other side, the far right of the theological spectrum. Out of sight right.

The major players in the developing Evangelical Movement were Billy Graham and the evangelistic phenomenon that captured the imagination of the church in the 1940s and 1950s that gave evangelicalism a national platform, and scholars like Harold John Ockenga and Carl Henry who provided the intellectual and educational credentials. *Uneasy Conscience of Modern Fundamentalism* provided the spark that became a roaring flame. *Christianity Today* emerged as the official publication.

The Evangelical Movement provided a needed corrective, a third option, a middle way, and it proved to be well received at the grassroots of the Christian church in North America.

Our own tribe, The Wesleyan Church, as well as our other American Holiness Movement cousins, saw ourselves as a subset within the larger movement. And true to our needy spirits, we saw ourselves as somehow "less than" compared to everyone else around us. As an "old" evangelical, I have lived through most of the development of this movement and watched it move from a highly respected movement to an embarrassed movement (anybody remember the television preachers – Jim and Jerry and Jimmy?) to now a voting-block movement courted by hopeful politicians.

It has seemed to have lost its way and ground to a halt. Lampooned by the left, not conservative enough for the far right, highjacked by the Church Growth Movement, dismissed as suspect and compromised by the younger church folk, a mystery to the media. As a young man, I saw it up close from the inside. Now as it has moved past me and left me wondering where it went, I see it from the outside, as it seems to be approaching its "post" life. Looking back, I have a confession to make. I became an "evangelical" out of embarrassment. Evangelical was much cooler than my native label, "holiness". I never gave up my holiness theological orientation or understanding. Just the label. I found other ways to say it.

I was embarrassed by the excesses of the American Holiness Movement and drawn to the respectability of a more balanced approach. Being embarrassed by my church family and sliding over to the more palatable group was a mistake for me, and in my later years I have dragged that sin out into the light, pointed at it and called it what it is – pride – and walked away from it. I am now back to being a "holiness" preacher . . . in the proper understanding of that word, mind you. That would be without the baggage.

For grounding perspective in understanding our place in the larger movement, I keep going back to our exiled Wesleyan prophet, Don Dayton, and his word of prophecy to The Wesleyan Church at a sidebar meeting at our 2012 General Conference (exiled prophets don't get the main stage). Don's reminder to us was, "We are not 'liberals' although we hold many views that could be considered liberal. We are not 'conservatives' although most of our constituency would identify as that. We are called to be 'radical'." Those in the emerging generation are born for the Wesleyan worldview: a "radical" commitment to Head and Heart. We need to let them take us back to our roots.

In my opinion, the current state of evangelicalism is the natural outcome of the fatal flaw of Reformed theology and it's worldview that tends to emphasize the Head (truth) and ignore the Heart (experience). That leads to decisions rather than devotion, information without transformation, regeneration without sanctification.

Where were we Wesleyans when the Reformed folk were taking the field? Why were we not out there writing the counter narrative, teaching the deeper way, offering a better perspective from within the Evangelical Movement? I'll tell you where we were. We Wesleyans were too busy saving our little corner of the world and sanctifying our saints over and over. My generation of Wesleyans fell to the temptation of focusing only on the Heart.

Ironic. On the one hand, there are those who prided themselves on their intellect. They have now left us with a shallow church. And on the other hand, we have those (us) who prided themselves in their robust heart spirituality. They (we) have now also left us with a shallow church.

It seems, for whatever reason, there is a smile of Providence on our tribe right now. Is there hope emerging with this next generation? Church plants are thriving in places we haven't been for a while – college towns and urban centers, populated by energetic young pastors and people, riding a fresh new wave of the Spirit. In addition, one in four Wesleyans attends a church of 1000 or more. Something is happening.

Something needs to happen, and a compromised political movement is not the answer.

Anyone ready to get off the "political power train" and wait for the next train, a new Movement from God? Who will write this generation's *Uneasy Conscience of Modern Evangelicalism* to help get this thing going?

CHAPTER THIRTEEN

HOLINESS ECLIPSED

How The Wesleyan Church sold its Holiness birthright in order to become an Evangelical Church

THE BAPTISTIFICATION OF THE WESLEYAN CHURCH

This is a sad story.

I love the Baptists. I live in a state where there are more Baptists than people. We owe a lot to their influence driving back the forces of evil in our communities. But the Baptists need our deeper discipleship dimension to enrich and complement their evangelistic zeal. And I love the Evangelicals. I've been one for just short of fifty years. When that Movement was on target and rolling, it was great to be in that vanguard. Until it got co-opted by power hungry preachers who took a bite of the poison apple and politicians who see us simply as votes to be played. The problem we should have had with the Evangelicals, but didn't, is that they wanted to take us further without allowing us to take them deeper.

How did our transition from Holiness to Evangelical happen? One regrettable choice at a time that eventually became a pattern.

Among other things, instead of a full presentation of all the claims of the Gospel, we began a drift toward a one-dimensional gospel characterized by shallowness. Instead of godly sorrow leading to repentance, we slowly opted for gentle assimilation avoiding uncomfortable confrontation. We replaced "Blessed Assurance" with casual assumptions. Instead of tear stained altars we have opted for newcomer receptions. We quit singing testimony songs because too many of our people have had no deep life change to sing about.

Instead of a public affirmation of faith (the oldtimers walked the aisle or it didn't count – extra points if it was sawdust!), we now have raised hands with all eyes closed (we really should have followed the Baptists' public invitations on that one). Instead of seeking and finding the "lost", we became seeker sensitive and invited them to find us. We substituted a one-time decision in place of deeply devoted discipleship. We substituted fire escape insurance in place of the baptism with fire Jesus promises and provides. We substituted information in place of transformation. We substituted signing up in place of praying through. We substituted sitting in a classroom in place of a robust and rowdy walk in the wild places led by the Holy Spirit.

We substituted cheap grace in place of sanctifying grace. We substituted a one-trip salvation response in place of a long and purifying walk with God. We substituted the spiritual equivalent of children's sparklers in place of *Lightning Bolts from Pentecostal Skies*.

I could go on. We traded deep and wide for bigger faster. Okay, one more. We substituted quick check response cards in place of the deep conversion of the soul.

And that's how it happened. We did a slow slide from who we were to who we've now become in too many of our churches. Not all, but too many. I understand what happened and why. I, and many of my Wesleyan friends, shifted and drifted from our roots to their respectability.

We messed up.

Our holiness cousin A.W. Tozer described where we found ourselves over time in way too many places when he wrote, "It is a solemn thing, and not a small scandal in the kingdom, to see God's children starving while actually seated at the Father's table." There was all that glorious bounty laid out in front of us, and we chose instead to sit down next to Esau and sell our birthright for a shallow bowl of tepid, tasteless, non-offensive, one-dimensional, spiritually watered-down, see-through soup. It might as well have been from a red and white Campbell's Soup can. The more and better and deeper has been there for us all the time. We just walked away from it.

It's not the Baptists who are to blame. It's not the Evangelicals who were our problem. We Wesleyans were our problem. If we had fulfilled our role of living in the power of the Holy Spirit – much different than the power of politics – and calling people to a deeper walk in the Spirit, and living a robust life of holiness in a way that made people believe it could be done, by the presence of the Holy Spirit in our lives, and going under the anointing of the Holy Spirit into the places our mommas told us never to go, our history would be significantly different. We could have fueled the Evangelical Movement with the imparted righteousness that changes the hearts and lives of people who then go out and change the world.

But we didn't.

We settled down. We sought safety and security. We simply weren't in the places where we were needed most desperately. We were supposed to be complementary to these other groups. But we allowed ourselves to be compromised in our calling and we ended up being near clones of the Baptists and consumed by the Evangelicals. So the problem I have is with us. I have a problem with me.

We messed up. We have done well as Evangelicals but we missed it on our special calling.

But those who have eyes to see and ears to hear know this is the True Wesleyan Moment. This time is our time. Inductive in nature, experiential in orientation, less noggin and more heart, making a different kind of difference in the world. The post-modern wanderer should be drawn to us, if we are true to who we were created to be – the "other" story, the story of Hope in Darkness, Depth of Experience, Sincerity of Heart, Purity of Motive, Optimistic Grace and Amazing Love. Incarnated. Filled to overflowing. Available. Sacrificial in spirit. Humble. And totally dependent on the power, presence, purification and propulsion of the Holy Spirit. There are a lot of those post-modern folks wandering around looking for us.

So maybe the new question is less "Where in the world did The Wesleyan Church go?" and more "Where in the world is The Wesleyan Church going?" Can The Wesleyan Church live in the mission of the Father's heart, in hot pursuit of the Risen Savior, set ablaze by the Holy Spirit? Can The Wesleyan Church reclaim its heritage of invading instead of just inviting? Can The Wesleyan Church shine in this culture like a city on a hill?

What I am saying will sound to some like a call to go back to the good old days. That's not what this is at all. This is a call to go forward into a new day and get this thing back on track. Let's pray this emerging generation can lead us out of the "Baptistification" of The Wesleyan Church we fell into, and back onto the higher road of a new "Wesleyanization" of The Wesleyan Church.

I can smell the smoke. Is there fire?

CHAPTER FOURTEEN

HOLINESS ECLIPSED

How The Wesleyan Church sold its Holiness birthright in order to become an Evangelical Church

THIS WAS MORE THAN A PHILOSOPHICAL SHIFT

When The Wesleyan Church made the shift from being a holiness church to being an evangelical church, we made more than a philosophical shift. We made a theological shift.

Always in our history, we were oriented toward the Third Person in the Trinity, the Holy Spirit. Martin Luther's criticism of the inner light pietists of his day, that they swallowed the Holy Spirit, "feathers and all", would have been a legitimate description of us as well. We were holiness people. But when they rolled out the flashy new model, Evangelicalism, we bought it right off the showroom floor. And we shifted from being Spirit-driven to being Christ-centered. That's a theological shift. It is not a shift into heresy or even toward heresy, but it is a shift of theological understanding, preference and orientation.

Genetta Cockrell Herrera introduced the book, *3 Colors of Ministry: A Trinitarian Approach to Identifying and Developing Your Spiritual Gifts*, by Kristin Schwarz of *Natural Church Development* fame, to the process The Wesleyan Church uses for assessing potential church planters. It was my first exposure to the book, and it was enlightening. The basic premise of the book is that individuals, local churches and even denominations tend to see things from one of three perspectives – the perspective of the Father, the perspective of the Son, or the perspective of the Holy Spirit. Whatever your Trinitarian orientation, so is your understanding of the church and its mission. And so also can you discover your blind spots. Since we are so prone to take sides, I suppose, we have a tendency to prefer one Person over the other in our view of the church and the world.

The Father-centered church tends to place its primary focus on love. It sees the Father as loving and it sees itself as a channel of that love to the world. This is, of course, a totally valid way of viewing the Father and the church, as well as the individual's calling to love our neighbor as we love ourselves. When this church or person goes wrong, it is usually in the direction of theological liberalism, marked by pluralism that sees no distinction between the Father God of the scriptures and any other "loving" religious diety or philosophy or ethic that can be found in the world. At some point, every decision is passed through the cognitive grid of "tolerance" and any position or teaching that seems to make an exclusionary claim is not tolerated.

The Christ-centered church tends to place its primary focus on truth. It sees Christ as the scripture describes him, the embodiment of truth – a truth to be known, a truth to be believed, a truth to be proclaimed. The Christ-centered church or person sees itself a channel of that truth to the world. This is a legitimate and valid way of viewing Christ and his mission in the world. And the Christ-centered church or person is to share that truth in a knowledgeable and informed way through any number of avenues, including personal witnessing. When this person or church goes wrong, it is usually in the direction of sterility. The faith is reduced to an accepted set of terms and orthodox statements, and that sometimes cools the life right out of the church and the believer. Formulas and mechanics take over.

The Spirit-driven church focuses on being led by the Spirit, being empowered by the Spirit, being informed by the Spirit. There is an openness to the unexplainable and the miraculous, and an expectation of the unexpected. The Spirit-driven church sees itself as being given a direct order to interfere with the world. This is definitely the edgier of the options, but it is New Testament endorsed and totally legitimate. This church or individual is to live with an ear open to the direction of the Holy Spirit and is called to obedience to those promptings. When this person or church goes wrong, it is usually in the direction of the flesh. Promptings that are not of the Spirit, or impressions that are of another spirit, or the impure motives of a darkened heart can be represented as being of the Spirit of God and create confusion, corruption, and crashes and burns.

The Pilgrim Holiness and Wesleyan Methodist Churches were unapologetically Spirit-driven in their theological orientation.

The early Pilgrims prayed for and expected divine healings. Their early leaders, Seth C. Rees and Martin Wells Knapp, were influenced by A.B. Simpson's Fourfold Gospel – salvation, sanctification, healing and the Second Coming. It was at the core of who they were. The Wesleyan Methodists were in the same camp. When we were good, we were really good. People got saved and delivered from sin and sinful habits. People were brought into a deeper relationship with God through the sanctifying filling of the Holy Spirit. People testified of divine healing. And everybody was all-in on getting their friends and family into a right relationship with God before the Lord returned.

My saintly grandmother was diagnosed with cancer. It was bad news. This was in the 1950s when there were few medical options. She was taken to the Holzier Clinic in Gallipolis, Ohio, ninety miles from our hometown. The folks back home gathered at the church, anointed a cloth with oil and prayed over it. The pastor brought the anointed cloth to her hospital room. She placed it on her body in faith that the Lord was going to heal her. When they x-rayed her prior to surgery, they called for the old x-rays. Something wasn't right. The tumor that had been there and was showing plainly on the old x-ray was mysteriously missing from the new one. She lived in great health for thirty more years after that.

That's why I pray every day for my friends with cancer – Willbo, Mike and Michael, John and Jim, Charles and Charles and Chris, Ola and Emily, Allison and Dallas, Donna and Robin, Kim and Carolyn, Deanna and Dacia, Joy and Sue, Pat and Naomi. My dear friend Steve used to be on this list, but he got healed.

Don't get me wrong. We still believe this. We never left this behind. But we left something behind. We decided we would rather be a little more respectable, a little less on the outside looking in. We became uneasy with the unpredictability and the emotion, a little more comfortable with the structured and controllable. We did not walk away from God or his blessings, but we walked away from our specific calling and became just another evangelical church. They rolled the shiny new model out in front of us. We climbed in and drove away.

For me, I think we already have enough of those kinds of churches. I think we need to trade in that model that is now old, worn out and broken down. Let's go get something that may not be so flashy, but will take us deeper and farther than our current generations have experienced.

Being a child of the muscle car era, I am wondering what would be today's spiritual equivalent of yesterday's '69 Chevy SuperSport?

CHAPTER FIFTEEN

HOLINESS ECLIPSED

How The Wesleyan Church sold its Holiness birthright in order to become an Evangelical Church

ABSTINENCE AND MODERATION

One of the indicators that we have shifted from being a holiness church to being an evangelical church has been our slow accommodation in attitude toward the use of beverage alcohol by our people.

There is not one single Holiness body in North America that has not held, by rule and practice, that the use of beverage alcohol is an unacceptable lifestyle choice for holiness people. This has been a historical, unwavering conviction from the beginning, universally accepted by the churches that composed the American Holiness Movement. It has been one of our defining marks as a movement. Not so much so for evangelical churches, many of whom take a position of moderation on this issue.

Will moderation be the "biblical" standard for beverage alcohol consumption in The Wesleyan Church going forward?

The current conversation in The Wesleyan Church about our historic stand for total abstinence from beverage alcohol seems to begin from this question, raised by our younger folks, whom we treasure, love and adore, and who, I believe, are honest in their questions: Why are we so out of step with the rest of our culture by insisting on maintaining this arcane tradition of restriction from consuming beverage alcohol?

The argument goes like this: The Bible clearly teaches moderation. Paul clearly advocated the use of alcohol for health reasons. Even Jesus endorsed imbibing – from his first miracle, to him being accused of being a wine-bibber, to the wine in the cup at the Last Supper. Eventually someone says, "Because of all of this, Jesus couldn't even be a member of The Wesleyan Church!" The conversation then continues to the real dilemma we face with this stand: Are we placing unnecessary impediments in the way of people from this alcohol-saturated culture who are seeking Christ through our ministries but don't understand our position on this issue? The trump card is then played. If the Bible endorses moderate use of alcoholic beverages, then our abstinence stance is unbiblical.

That's a pretty good argument.

I would like to start the discussion one step back from that first question, however, by addressing the assumption of moderation as the stated "biblical" position, to see if the argument has merit.

My starting question would be: Why would the scriptures put forth an acceptance of moderate consumption of beverage alcohol instead of an insistence on abstaining? Is it a matter of principle, or is it a circumstantial accommodation?

I will just go on and state my assumption right out front: I do not believe the reasons for alcohol consumption in the first century Middle East culture can be equated with the practice of alcohol consumption in twenty-first century North America. The moderation argument has to assume this or there is no argument. "They did it, so it must be okay. Why can't we do it?"

Let me illustrate what I mean when I say it isn't the same thing. If you were a first century consumer, could you walk into a supermarket in downtown Jerusalem and go to an eighty-foot long aisle of shelves stocked full of every imaginable option of beverage alcohol? Could you walk into the refrigerated beer cave and get any assortment of beer anyone ever dreamed of? And I'm not even talking about the hard stuff here.

In North Carolina we have state-controlled "ABC Stores" for that – entire free-standing Alcohol Beverage Control buildings stocked with liquor. No, you could not enjoy the variety of options in beverage alcohol in first century Jerusalem that we "enjoy" in the worldly metropolis of

Kernersville. It's a totally different scenario driven by totally different circumstances.

But even more to the point, if you lived in first century Jerusalem could you walk into the supermarket downtown and choose from a multiplicity of non-alcohol options – whole aisles dedicated to soft drinks, a section for sports drinks, more juice options than a first century person could imagine, a solid wall of milk products, and all kinds of bottled water options? No. But we don't even have to go to the store to beat the options of our first century friends. In North America, we can just walk over to the sink or the refrigerator water dispenser and draw cool, clear, clean water we can drink with no fear of contamination (with the exception of a few unfortunate places).

So, that means if you live in first century Jerusalem and wine is your best safe option then wine is what you're drinking. An acknowledgment of that in scripture is not the same as an endorsement. It's just someone reporting on first century realities that were part of first century life. It was a necessary reality, not a recreational option.

But is it really "biblical"? Biblical as a qualification should mean something that is clearly taught as a truth in scripture trustworthy for life and doctrine, not something that is mentioned incidentally in scripture. A mention of something in the text is not an automatic endorsement of that action or concept. So the bottom line question for us is not, "Is moderation 'biblical' and abstinence 'unbiblical'?", but since we have choices they did not have, which choice is the best reflection of the kind of life laid out for the fully devoted disciple of Christ in scripture? Which choice is the wisest choice? Which choice draws me closer to the character Christ desires to develop in me by his personal presence in my life, the Holy Spirit? Which choice is a truly biblical choice?

In my opinion, if you're going to promote moderation as the standard going forward for a holiness church based on the spirit of scripture, you need to get another argument. This "biblical" one doesn't work.

Let me ask some other questions.

Why is beverage alcohol such a hot button issue for us right now? If you write an opinion for Wesleyans on the internet on overeating, or tobacco, or marijuana, or gambling, or wasting time, how many comments would you get? If you wrote an opinion for or against beverage alcohol, how many comments would you get? Why is that?

We do all understand, right, that abstinence from beverage alcohol has nothing to do with our salvation? We know in itself, our decision to imbibe or abstain does not determine our standing before God. It's not "saved if we don't" or "damned if we do", right? I'm not talking about going against "light" here. I'm saying that keeping a law does not save us.

Do we also understand that in the process of our sanctification, keeping that same law does not make us holy? As we respond to the leadership of the Holy Spirit, in these matters of lifestyle and behavior, the Holy Spirit is working in the area of our sanctification. Do we understand it is his work in our lives that produces righteousness in us through our surrender? And our living in that obedience is not the cause of our sanctification but the fruit of it?

Some ask, "Then why can't we just let the Holy Spirit be our guide? Why do we have to try to add things to it?" (meaning rules, guides, helps, lists). So I ask, is the inner voice of the Holy Spirit the only guide we are given? Does God not also guide through scripture? Or godly counsel? Or circumstances? Or through the benefits of long and consistent obedience? Or through the painful experiences of disobedience? Has our Creator not given us a brain? How about through the collective conscience of a group of likeminded believers? Does the Holy Spirit not faithfully work through all these avenues and more?

If a group of likeminded believers, then, led by the Holy Spirit's influence through inner impressions, scripture, counsel, common experience, and reason discovers that they are in agreement on a number of issues and write it down on a piece of paper, is that legitimate or not? If it is, what would you call it?

Do you suppose it is possible that, if you find yourself in harmony with such an agreement, you might add your endorsement to it by calling it by a noble name such as a "covenant" or a "commitment" or even "helps and guides to holy living"? And if a person happened not to agree fully with the agreement, do you suppose that person might be tempted to try to discredit whatever point is in question by calling it by a less noble name like a "rule"? Or labeling it "legalistic"? Or, if they really wanted to drop the bomb on the other crowd, accuse them of being "pharisaical" (read: acting like the enemies of Jesus)?

If that "agreement" is about the consumption of alcohol, and that agreement has had a unanimous acceptance in the group for more than 150 years, until relatively recently, wouldn't it be fair to ask, "What changed?" Did the nature of beverage alcohol change? Did the effects of beverage alcohol change?

What if the only thing that really changed from the outside was the amount of pressure put on the group from the alcohol-saturated culture around us pressuring us to accommodate? Should we do it? Should we let the pressure press us or should we be pressing back against the pressure?

What if the drive for change from the inside is coming on us because we are increasingly reaching people who are from other faith traditions or no faith tradition to whom abstinence is a totally foreign concept? How do we remain sensitive to that while leading them to a deeper relationship with Christ, without setting unnecessary stumbling blocks in their way? Do we change, or do we help them to change – over time and through a loving, caring discipleship process? Is it arrogant for us to talk about "helping them change", or are we called to be humble, empowered change agents in this world?

Are we not called to set apart Christ in our hearts as Lord, and always be ready to give an answer to anyone who asks us to give a reason for the hope that we have, in gentleness and with respect? As aggravating as this question may be to some, I have to ask it: Should we not consider what happens to our testimony to hope-challenged people if we imbibe a substance with intoxicating, addictive influence? What hope do we hold out for someone trapped in that intoxicating addiction? "Control yourself, man"?

95

Should we change our fundamental behavioral question from, "What is best?" to "What is okay?" Is that a better direction for us to take as a people?

Which direction will lead us to become more and more like Christ and less and less like the person we used to be? What manner of life should I live that will honor God the most? If I know the answer to that question, am I not honor bound to pursue it? How do we answer those questions as a holiness church compared to our answers as an evangelical church?

When The Wesleyan Church changed its membership structure at the 2016 General Conference, making membership entry level leading into a defined path of discipleship, one of the comments from detractors was, "Oh, so we can drink now." Not so. Entry level means we take newly converted people into our church fellowship, with their current practices and lifestyles and habits, and disciple them into mature Christians, helping them by the power of the Holy Spirit at work within them to shed the old life and enter into the new life with new and healthy and better practices and lifestyles and habits. We have not changed our opinion on beverage alcohol. We have not removed it from the list defining what the sanctified life looks like as illustrated by our "Helps and Guides to Holy Living" in the Constitution. We have not lifted this expectation as a lifestyle choice from the lives of our people. We have not lifted this expectation from our local church leaders. We have not lifted this prohibition from our credentialed ministers. Yet.

But, in my opinion, our slide from being a holiness church into being an evangelical church will be complete, if and when we do.

PART THREE

HOLINESS REDICOVERED

How The Wesleyan Church
Can Get Back What
We Gave Away

This is not about going back. This is about going forward.
This is not about sacrificing bigger to get better.
This is about getting bigger and better at the same time,
in pursuit of our best.

As much as I love E. Stanley Jones and his statement,
"We must go deeper before we go further",
this is about going deeper as we go further.

This is about "more".

CHAPTER SIXTEEN

HOLINESS REDICOVERED

How The Wesleyan Church Can Get Back
What We Gave Away

THE PATH FORWARD IS THREE STEPS FORWARD,
ONE STEP BACK

So how do we make the transition from an Evangelical Church back to a Holiness Church?

We do that by how we live a convincing life. We do that by how we preach to our people. We do that by how we call our people to a deeper walk. We do that by how we disciple our converts. We do that by how we evangelize our neighbors. We do that by how we focus our worship. We do that by how we live out our faith. We do that by how we sing a new song. We do that by how we handle temptation. We do that by how we avoid the mistakes of the past.

We do that by how we raise the awareness for ourselves and our people that there is an abundant, fulfilling, joyful life of full surrender that brings blessings beyond what we are able to think or imagine. And it comes at the initiative of our Heavenly Father through the gift of his Son and the abiding presence of his Holy Spirit within us. And it comes as we intentionally make space for him in our lives. It is a gift of his good, pleasing and perfect will in cooperation with our sacrifice of our will to him, a living sacrifice.

It is forgiveness, plus transformation. It is a life-changing decision, plus a life of devotion. It is a change of category, plus a change in character. It is us in Christ, plus Christ in us. To get theological about it, it is not just an imputed righteousness, but it is also and most importantly an imparted righteousness. It is "saved", plus "sanctified". The result is an infilling of God's love that reorients us away from selfishness to a profound love for God and others, and empowers us to make a different kind of difference in their lives – a difference with eternal dimensions to it, not just a temporary relief of their currently binding circumstances (but we need to address that, too).

In order to see this happen more fully and for it to become a more consistent characteristic of who we are in The Wesleyan Church, we need to take three steps forward after we take one step back.

First, we need to step around the American Holiness Movement and go back to Wesley. We need to fully understand and embrace the concept of love filling our hearts, expelling sin. We do not need to go back to the formulas and we need to walk away from the current shallowness. We need to get back to understanding sanctification as a relationship with a purpose.

We need to see our relationship with God like a healthy marriage. There are things you must do in order to be married and stay married. There are other things you can do as a married person, but they might not enrich your marriage if you choose to do them. So you should not do those things. Happy wife, happy life. There are other things that you should not do as a married person. Although they might not wreck your marriage, you can be sure you, husband, are going to pay the price if you do them. Just sayin'. Then there are things, if you do them, they will wreck your marriage and your marriage likely will not survive. You may damage it beyond repair.

It takes discipline to have a healthy marriage. Many times, when we hear the word "discipline", we think only of human effort and restrictive rules. And it can be just that. But godly disciplines are the Spirit-led and empowered actions flowing out of sanctified attitudes that keep a loving relationship alive and thriving.

To some who do not know the joy of a beautiful marriage relationship, these things may look like killjoy rules and they may scoff at the person choosing to abide by them. But to the man who lives for the joy he sees in the eyes of his wife, that joy is priceless to him. To the woman who delights in the rapture she sees in the countenance of her husband, there is no other way she wants to live. They are not impoverished. They are enriched.

A wife thrives in a marriage where she knows she can trust her husband with her very life. A husband thrives in a marriage where he knows he has no rivals. Marriages thrive when the people in them would rather die than see harm come to the other person. That relationship is built upon each one living for the good and happiness of the other.

Our relationship with God is like that only unbelievably better. We are in a relationship with a person who is perfect in every way, who is rich beyond measure, who is famously generous and reckless with his generosity, and who dances over us in love. And, beyond that, he releases his power into our lives to make us the kind of person who resembles him, although we are made of dust and he is not. The only thing that holds us back is our level of commitment to this relationship. That is the Wesleyan message of optimistic grace. That is the force that compelled the early Methodists not just to be happy about the condition of their own souls, but they could not rest until others enjoyed that same peace and joy.

We need to get back to that.

The path forward follows these three Wesleyan values. Salvation. Sanctification. Service.

Salvation

While Wesley declared that the doctrine of sanctification as found in the scriptures was the "Grand Depositum" of the Methodist movement, his recovery of the doctrine of the assurance of salvation was just as important in his day and ours. There are many things that we can declare that we believe are God's will. There is one thing indisputable, and that is that God is not willing that any should perish but that all should come to repentance. He said it himself. He sent his Son to live among us to show us what he is like and how serious he is about our salvation. As the Lamb who was slain before the very foundation of the world, Jesus willingly laid down his life for us, paid a debt on Calvary we could not pay, and carried our sins into the sea of God's forgetfulness. Corrie Ten Boom said he put a "No Fishing" sign there. I've never seen it but I don't doubt it.

The Wesleyan Church has always declared clearly and without apology, this wonderful truth. While other North American churches grew primarily through transfer growth (we did that, as well), The Wesleyan Church has consistently emphasized and celebrated growth by conversion. On any given Sunday in any given Wesleyan church, you will hear a clear and compelling presentation of the gospel. And it is not rare to see someone respond to the invitation to receive Christ, or hear someone share a testimony of coming to Christ through the witness of their Wesleyan neighbor or friend or family member.

I remember how we rejoiced in our District when we declared a "zero tolerance for zeroes" on the annual report line that gave the number of persons saved through local church ministries. Forty-five days from the reporting deadline our pastors received a message that said, "I know what you are doing is important, but if you are planning to report a zero on people saved this year, we would respectfully request that you stop whatever it is you are doing and go win someone to Christ. Then you can go back to doing whatever it was you were doing." Where we used to report 650 to 700 persons saved, we began to report over 3,000.

The Wesleyan Church has done a real good job of keeping the main thing the main thing. We do not need to let our foot off the gas on this.

Sanctification.

This is the process God uses to refine our character. From the Holiness Code of Leviticus to the white-robed righteous gathered around the Throne in the Book of Revelation, it is obvious what kind of people God desires and expects us – commands us even – to be. He is holy. He wants us to be holy.

We need to understand sanctification correctly.

It has two parts to it. One part is the understanding that we are set apart. When we enter into a relationship with God through Christ by the indwelling presence of the Holy Spirit, we are made a new creature with new expectations. Like a marriage, we are to belong exclusively to God. Old allegiances are passed away. Our new allegiance is to him only. When that starts is at our conversion, but as we grow, we become aware of competing claims within, and that needs to be resolved. As we surrender to his claims and sacrifice our claims, we enter into an ever- deepening relationship that allows him to recreate his character in us over time. This can begin with an instantaneous and climactic experience or it can be a matter of gradual growth. However it happens, it is more than just being forgiven. We are being transformed.

That's the second part. There is actually a power at work within us to change us. When we open our lives to this new and deeper relationship with God, we enter into a path of accelerated growth. It is a measurable growth. And there is a deeper compassion for others, a definite sense of purpose, and a new power over sin, internal and external, that is evidenced in increasing victory, consistent obedience, and compassionate love.

It is not perfection (sorry Mr. Wesley, but I understand you were sorry you ever used that term, also). We will always be human and subject to failure and falling. That doesn't go away. What does go away is the thirst for falling, the desire for falling, the life pattern characterized by falling. We find a new and stronger will to love God and others, to keep ourselves in our proper place under God, and to live a more consistent life of Christlike attitude and behavior. Our neighbors like us better, our spouse likes us better, our boss and co-workers like us better, our children like us better, even the family pets like us better.

In The Wesleyan Church, our path of discipleship for our people needs to be laid down upon this foundational doctrine. Discipleship is not sharing facts. Discipleship is a pathway of life leading to Christlikeness, not just by exposing people to truth (that's an important element), but by exposing them to The Truth who by his power transforms them. It is a process that produces a product: a fully devoted follower of Christ.

We need to experience sanctification completely.

The work that begins in us at our regeneration includes other concomitant blessings: justification, adoption, and initial sanctification. While God's work in us begins way before we are ever aware of it through his prevenient grace, his saving work in us begins at our conversion. We receive a restored relationship with our Heavenly Father (justification and adoption). We receive new life through what Christ did for us on the cross (regeneration). And we receive the personal purifying presence of God, the Holy Spirit, into our lives (initial sanctification).

This is to be followed by growth in grace. That is what sanctification is. All of us in Christ experience it. But there is a marvelous, too often untapped truth that we need to experience. We need to experience the abundant life Jesus talked about. We need to experience what the Father has promised that Jesus talked about. We need to experience the power from the Holy Spirit Jesus promised the disciples. We need to experience the fullness of God Paul talks about. We need to experience being sanctified through and through that Paul said was God's will for us. We need a fresh visitation of the Holy Spirit upon us that will take us deeper and further at the same time. We need a complete experience of this wonderful relationship with God.

We need to talk about sanctification clearly.

This deeper relationship with God does not need to be wrapped in mystery, and it does not need to be communicated in fog. It really is simple and easy to understand. It is relational and it is dynamic. It is not something we work up or try to make happen. It is inside out, not outside in.

We need to leave the technical terms for the textbooks and talk to our people in plain and simple language. We need to help them fall fully in love with God, not the doctrine. We need to help them fall fully in love with people, not causes or ideas. We need to help them live a carful life, not a weird one. We need to help them seek to grow in grace, and understand this is not about perfect performance. We need to help them seek for more love, not just power. We need to help them make it about him and them, not about themselves. We need to help them seek to go deeper as they go further. We need to get them off their seat and into the street. We need to engage their heart, not just their head. We need to teach them to have the courage to wait on God, and not impatiently try to make things happen in their own strength. We need to teach them to have total confidence in the power of the Spirit, and no confidence in the flesh. We need to help them let humility reign and pride be crucified. We need to teach them how to value freedom, and avoid bondage. We need to help them understand the importance of avoiding a condemning spirit. We need to teach them to keep short accounts with God and others, and to apologize quickly and often. We need to teach them to learn to say "Yes" to God and "No" to temptation. And if they get caught up in Second Coming teachings, we need to teach them to stop waiting for Jesus to return and get out there in the world where he is waiting for them.

Then we can put them on the Witness Stand in our worship services, either through a live testimony or a previously recorded video, and let them tell their sanctification story. The more of these deeper life conversations we have with our people or in the presence of our people, the more we will fan the flame of holiness among us. Our leaders need to intentionally talk about this to our people.

We need to sing about sanctification consistently.

I spoke about J.D. Walt earlier. You may not know this, but in another life he was an early mentor to contemporary Christian artist, Chris Tomlin. They have maintained a close relationship with each other, and for a long time J.D.'s wife, Tiffany, was Chris Tomlin's manager.

One of the things that burdens J.D., and me as well, is that we have almost abandoned the Christian song writing field in North America to people who see God and the world through the Reformed theology lens. They write beautiful, uplifting and inspiring songs. But almost all of their songs are majesterial in nature. They magnify the majesty of God, and he is worthy to be praised above all. But there is plenty of room left for testimony songs that exalt the Lord's work in our lives. Especially his sanctifying work. The Wesley brothers filled the air with such songs. They lived in a majesterial era as well, and were roundly criticized for stepping outside the Psalms and writing both original texts and music, and setting text to popular tunes. Some 6,000-plus songs later, they had the whole world singing.

We don't have to sing their songs, although many still survive in popularity to this day. But we should have a song to sing. A deeper song than some we are singing today. A song that rises out of our sanctified hearts and bursts forth from our sanctified lips about the sanctifying power of our glorious God. What would happen if a number of our younger artists gathered in a songwriters' incubator on a regular basis and either rewrote some Wesley hymns or authored some original holiness compositions?

We need to understand sanctification correctly. We need to experience sanctification completely. We need to talk about sanctification clearly. We need to sing about sanctification consistently. And we need to take sanctification outside the walls compassionately.

That is actually the third step forward on our path, along with salvation and sanctification.

Service

I have probably said enough about this, especially in the treatment of The Second Half of the Second Half of the Gospel. It is important, in my way of thinking, that we refuse to settle down, happy to be happy in the Lord, and fail to understand that the only reason God desires to have a sanctified people is so he can use them in his mission in the world. That's all.

His work of sanctification in our lives empowers us and compels us to work until Jesus comes to see the whole world know him and love him like we know him and love him. It gets us out of the way, puts him in his rightful place in our lives, and gives us the opportunity to fulfill his purpose for our lives. And we don't have to be part of a big church to be a part of his solution in the world. The big box churches may well be around in the American ecclesiastical landscape for a good while – and I hope they are – but it seems that one of the places where the new wine is bubbling with vitality is in the smaller, more organic, infiltrated church where the younger generation is finding a brand of church they always believed could be, but have never really seen until now.

What if we help them understand the sanctified life in a way that allows them to experience even more of the power of God matched up with their deep commitment to change the world? What if we help them understand the sanctified life in a way that confirms in them and their friends that God has a clear and compelling purpose for their lives and their church? What if we help them understand the sanctified life in a way that convinces them that they are chosen by God for this time in this place to work through his power and direction to make all the difference for someone who may never be reached otherwise?

Sometimes when I think of us, I think of the ancient Israelites. They were so proud to be God's chosen people. As I read their story, I am often tempted to ask, "Did you ever stop to ask what you were chosen for?" I know that's not very nice, but God has a purpose way beyond us. For them, it was to bring into the world at the appointed time the Savior of the world. I'm not sure they ever quite got that. For us, it is to bring into our world – our sphere of influence – the Savior of the world. By the power of God invested in us through the Holy Spirit, let us rediscover our holiness heritage in a way that depopulates hell and fills heaven full.

Salvation. Sanctification. Service. Those are the steps forward for The Wesleyan Church.

CHAPTER SEVENTEEN

HOLINESS REDICOVERED

How The Wesleyan Church Can Get Back
What We Gave Away

A JEWISH PERSPECTIVE ON HOLINESS

"There is an ethic by which we are to live, but the ethic has to be preceded by the encounter. There is no ethic without the encounter."

These are the words spoken to me by Josh LeRoy, one of the most broadly read persons I know. He was talking about the Jewish ethical discipline called *mussar* (moos-ahr'). It means "ethic" or "discipline" or "instruction" or even "chastisement", depending on the context. It can even be understood as a "way of holiness". It is a system of life that, rather than being rules-based like most Jewish systems, is values-based. Instead of outwardly imposed requirements being expected to make us better people and bring us closer to God, *mussar* works from the inside out.

Based on the ethical teachings of the Torah, *Mussar* as a movement traces its roots to tenth and eleventh century Judaism and the teachings of Rabbi Saddiah Gaon in Babylon (modern Iraq) who wrote, *The Book of Beliefs and Opinions*, and Rabbi Bahya Ibn Pakudah in Spain who wrote, *Duties of the Heart*. The teachings are not scripture, but they are based in scripture. The word, *mussar*, appears fifty-one times in the Old Testament text, most of them in the Book of Proverbs.

In an article titled, "What Is *Mussar*? A History and Overview of this Virtues-Based Approach to Jewish Ethics", author Greg Marcus describes *mussar* as a Jewish spiritual practice that gives concrete instructions on how to live a meaningful and ethical life, in answer to the challenge, "Why is it so hard to be good?"

Josh LeRoy explains that by cultivating the inner virtues, as opposed to the strict adherence to a set of rules, the Jewish practitioners of *mussar* believe outward obedience will naturally follow behind. It is understood to be a way to holiness and a way of holiness. The inner virtues *mussar* seeks to cultivate are, in this order, humility, patience, gratitude, compassion, order, equanimity, honor, simplicity, enthusiasm, silence, generosity, truth, moderation, loving-kindness, responsibility, trust, faith, and *yirah* (reverence). It is easy to trace the biblical roots of this list of virtues, not unlike the fruit of the Spirit in the New Testament. Again, this is not scripture, but it is based in scripture. It is not Christian, but the virtues describe the character of Christ.

Ibn Pakudah made this interesting statement that will grab the attention of New Testament holiness believers. "The very basis for an act ... depends on the intentions and inner life of the heart."

Marcus observed that those attempting to master this ethical way of living ran into a problem. They "recognized that simply learning about kindness does not make us more kind. Moreover, they understood that our inner drives, wounds and appetites often manifest as the *yetzer hara* (the evil inclination), actively preventing us from behaving as we know we should."

It is good to see things from another perspective sometimes. It gives us a fresh, new look at something familiar from a whole different angle. In *mussar*, this path of ethical behavior, I hear these holiness echoes.

First, there is a beautiful testimony in this of the yearning of the heart to know God, walk in fellowship with God, be like God in character, and please God through our actions. That is part of the effaced *Imago Dei* that continues to exist in every human ever born. The theologians who teach the concept of total depravity are wrong. There is a grace, prevenient grace, which goes before saving grace and manifests itself in a drawing toward God and a desire to know God. That is what drives *mussar*.

Second, it is a universal experience that becomes an exercise in futility to try to live this life without the enabling power of God. The spirit is willing, but that old *yetzer hara* operating in the flesh is a constant downward pull frustrating the highest desires and best efforts of the religious, and a constant deceiver substituting selfish pride of accomplishment in place of all those virtuous desires. All of us have a common problem. We all have sinned and fallen short of the glory of God. Paul's wretched man – "Who will rescue me from this body of death?" – is the person who tries to handle sin and attain righteous in his or her own strength. It's not going to happen, no matter how much *mussar* we try to muster.

Third, there is way. It is the way of holiness which may very well be much like the way of *mussar*. The difference between this life and the life of the "wretched man" is, in this way a Friend has offered to walk this path with us, to say to us, "this is the way, walk in it." A Friend has offered to live within us, to abide in power and purity in our hearts. A Friend has conquered the power of sin and offers to break the power of the *yetzer hara* that is so inclined to evil. A Friend has offered to fill us with the essence of his character, holy love. That's who he is. And that's who we are, in him.

Holiness people can readily identify with the struggles represented in *mussar*. Greg Marcus quotes one *mussar* teacher, Rabbi Elya Lopian, as explaining the struggle this way, the challenge of "teaching the heart what the mind already understands." In that statement is the challenge every religion faces – the inability of rules to transform the heart, and the inability of religion to replicate the dynamic of relationship with a living and life-transforming God. To be fair to the practitioners of *mussar*, theirs is a heartfelt effort to relate to the Living God from the heart, and I cannot imagine that somehow the Living God does not respond to that. We'll let God keep the score on that. That's his business, not ours. But our sad story in the American Holiness Movement is that too often, we tried to substitute a rules-based ethic for true holiness.

You can take a person who decides to live a "holy" life and he or she can begin by the power of their will to emulate and imitate the characteristics of holiness.

They can develop a list of those characteristics and live by them consistently. They can improve over time in their consistency. They can even find other people who are on the same path. Or they can co-exist among people who are on the true path. They believe they are making themselves holy and thus acceptable to God and helpful to others by the imposition of these disciplines from the outside (disciplines which are valid and scriptural by the way). And to the human eye, they sure look like who they claim to be.

Then you can take a person who falls in love with God through what they see in Christ, and by the power of the Holy Spirit, they surrender to his work in their life. They begin a journey where over time and at his pace, they become more and more like Christ and less and less like the person they used to be. This inner life will definitely work its way out in this person's actions, attitudes and relationships. It will be authentic and genuine and refreshing.

Here's the deal.

You can stand these two people side-by-side and they will look identical. But the legalism of the first person will eventually betray them, many times in jealousy or a judgmental or critical attitude toward the second person. The first person is rooted in pride. The second is rooted in righteousness. The first person is trying to live a life that is unsustainable while the second person is sustained by the abiding presence and power of the Holy Spirit.

God is too merciful to allow the first person to continue down his or her path because it is leading them to destruction, so he takes away whatever fulfills them and lets them dry up until their thirst brings them in humility back to him. Many times he must resort to bringing about a public deflation in order to bring about his redemptive change. We know them. Our hearts break for them. Their fall was so public and cataclysmic. And we pray to God it does not happen to us. God does not care one bit about our reputation. He only cares about our redemption. He will trash our reputation if that is what it takes to redeem us. Fortunately for us, God doesn't care about his reputation either. As my dad used to say, God is not proud. If he was, he wouldn't have any of us!

In our scenario the life of the first person is a life of legalism. There is a way that seems right to us, but it ends in destruction. The life of the second person leads to true holiness that glorifies God, blesses my neighbor, and will not be satisfied until everyone – no matter how lost for how long – also knows how long and how wide and how high and how deep is the love of God.

There is no short cut to sanctification. It is a long and winding road. But it leads to life. That other road is downhill all the way and it ends in a dark and lonely place. But God is always there, in mercy saying, "Follow me."

Holy Spirit inhabited *mussar*. This is the way. Walk in it.

CHAPTER EIGHTEEN

HOLINESS REDICOVERED

How The Wesleyan Church Can Get Back
What We Gave Away

TO BE IS BETTER THAN TO SEEM

I was eleven years old. It was Sunday night, so we were at church. The pastor had given an invitation to come forward and pray at the altar at the close of the service. Three people responded, two over on the left and one on the right. I was among the group praying for the person on the right. The folks where I was kneeling finished praying and returned to their seats. I remained where I was, continuing in prayer for the people on the left.

Sister Kiser, seeing me kneeling by myself, assumed I was there as a seeker, and she came over to me and asked, "Do you want to be sanctified?" I had no idea what that woman was talking about, but I knew a good little boy would answer "yes" to that kind of question. I said, "Yes." She called for others to gather in prayer. "Danny Gene wants to be sanctified." Several gathered to pray. I'm confident they were thinking, "He's eleven years old, for crying out loud." But they prayed.

When we were finished and I got to my feet, I still did not know what it was that I did not have, but now I was fully aware that I did not have it. My pastor met me in the center aisle, got on eleven year old eye level with me, and asked, "Honey, did you get satisfied?" I tearfully nodded my head no. He said, "Well, you can be!" And he put his hands on my shoulders and lit in praying, and the glory fell!

I felt like lightning had hit me right in the heart. I did what any eleven year old boy would do if he gets hit by lightning. I took off running. I ran between the pews, down the side aisle, across the front of the church, and back up the center aisle. I nearly tackled the pastor as I jumped into his arms. I still had no idea what it was I had, but I knew without a shadow of a doubt, whatever it was, I had it. I got the full dose!

It would not be very wise to try to build a theological construct out of my experience with the expectation that every Christian in the world, for all time, should experience exactly what I experienced in the Westwood Christian Baptist Church that night. And I never experienced anything like that at any other time in my life since then. What I have experienced, however, is something that every Christian in all the world for all time should and could experience. That is a fulfilling, growing, enriching relationship with God through Christ by the power and presence of the Holy Spirit who has faithfully walked with me every step of my journey – loving me, forgiving me, directing me, protecting me, empowering me, transforming me, using me, and stretching me. And this will go on forever.

As I have opened my life to him, he has filled every space I have given him. And he has brought into my life a wonderful number of fellow pilgrims who are on the same path, and they have enriched my life, as well. They made me hungry for more of God.

Most often, we come to holiness through what we see in the lives of other people. These are some of the people God placed in my life to live a real version of holiness before me. God used them to draw me closer to himself and convince me that this life was legitimate, desirable and by his help livable. They were nowhere near perfect in their performance (which was actually a good thing), but they loved God with all their hearts.

Fred and Elizabeth were my godly grandparents. As young adults they surrendered their lives completely to the Lord, became founding members of a small holiness denomination in the Ohio River Valley, and through thick and thin, lived blamelessly before me.

Holly Conley (father of John Conley, past President of Circleville Bible College now Ohio Christian University) was my boyhood pastor. Humble, holy and sincere, he helped me fall in love with Jesus.

Aunt Maggie was a poor widow in our church in my teen years. One sister was the wife of a highly renowned holiness evangelist, another was a flamboyant and forceful woman known throughout her District for her personality, and a brother was a wealthy farmer with a generous heart. But Maggie had something none of the other three possessed. She lived a life of poverty, totally dependent on God to sustain her, and as a result his glory and joy shined out of her life in a special way. That impacted me beyond words.

Sonnie was a friend of our family who loved and lived for God. I was there the night God powerfully called her to overseas mission service, in one of those transcendent moments where the presence of God filled the tabernacle where we were all praying. It was a once-in-a-lifetime experience that I never got over and never expect to.

Jack was a young preacher full of the Spirit, a generation ahead of me. God used him in a camp meeting service to speak profoundly into my life and reconfirm my call to ministry as a sixteen year old when I was wondering if I could really do this. "It was just a bush. But God was in the bush and that is what made all the difference."

Raymond was my District Superintendent hero when I was in college and seminary. God used him to help me understand, in his words, "Holiness and humility are twins." They always go together. They are inseparable.

James was my college professor and academic dean. I caused that man so much grief by my laziness and lateness. But he saw something in me he was willing to invest in, by the power of the Holy Spirit in his life. I doubt he ever thought I would end up pastoring his home church, and later becoming his District Superintendent. He walked patiently alongside me all those years.

Ransom was a sweet-spirited, anointed Wesleyan Methodist evangelist who impacted me profoundly as a college student. I came home for the weekend, and he was there for a Revival. After the service, I was sitting in the parsonage den reading the paper and suddenly my foot was being lifted up, and there was this spiritual giant on his knees, shining my shoes, and weeping as he did so.

114

Don was one of my seminary professors. The fullness of the Spirit dwelled in him. At a time when I was going under, God used "a word from the Lord" through him to rescue me.

Keith was very instrumental in developing me into a leader. He had a life-changing encounter with God in the mountains of Colorado and came back on fire. He led a movement of young leaders that impacts The Wesleyan Church to this day. And beyond. I got swept up in it and it set the direction for the rest of my life.

Percy was an evangelist a couple of generations ahead of me. He was so full of the scriptures that he was known as "The Walking Bible". I was his pastor at the end of his life. When others of his generation were severe in their spirit and grew old and hard and bitter, I watched him grow sweeter and sweeter. He was the real deal.

Helen was our pianist in one of the churches I pastored. There was no one who exhibited the fruit of the Spirit like Miss Helen (not always the case with church pianists). Yet she struggled with her assurance that she was truly sanctified. Why? Because her experience came to her in a gradual progression of growth, not in a lightning bolt experience like it was supposed to. That helped me determine to tear down the "only one way to get it" mindset that is not true to the Bible and is not true to life.

Preston was a Spirit-filled prophet. His eyes just blazed when the Spirit was on him. I was present in the room of a dear friend who was battling cancer. Preston led us in prayer. The glory fell in that room with such power that had the man been dead, I believe he would have sprung to life. A young pastor just doesn't get over that kind of thing.

Floyd was my vice-chairman and my best friend in one of our churches – a great combination for a young pastor in over his head. There was nothing dramatic about Floyd. You just knew you were in the presence of a man of God when you were with this rock-solid saint.

Johnnie was a prayer warrior. I was in a tough spot, needing God's grace and strength, feeling totally inadequate to negotiate hotel and conference contracts for an area youth convention. I called home early that morning to ask Cynthia to call Mr. Johnnie to pray for me. She called back immediately and said, "Mr. Johnnie told me he got up off his knees praying for you, to answer the phone. He said to tell you everything's going to be all right." And it was. So much so that the General Manager of the host hotel was dumbfounded by the contract and was ready to fire his Convention Manager!

John was a world-renowned Scottish preacher with a wonderful story and a heart to match. His emphasis on falling in love with Jesus all over again brought me to a whole new level of relationship with the Lord.

Melba is a sweet, saintly woman on Harkers Island who is a prayer warrior. She and her husband Billy raised three ornery boys, Kerry, Billy Joe and Stephen. They tried their best to be rascals but they didn't have a chance. She prayed them right into the kingdom and straight into the ministry! And she has prayed for me and my ornery boys many a time, too.

Chlora was my aunt, my Mom's oldest sister. For the first several decades of her life, she was cold, hard and far from God. But in her later years, God gloriously broke through, filled her with his Spirit, and turned her into a woman powerful in prayer. Where she used to be the bad girl in the family, she became our go-to option when we needed God's help – even if it was a pair of blue Nike athletic shoes young Josh had his heart set on but could not find. "Call Aunt Chlora," he implored. We did reluctantly. She began praying. We walked around the corner and there they were. I really don't think it was about the shoes at all. I think it was about honoring the faith of a little boy, and teaching him early that God cares.

Aron, Buddy and Keith are Spirit-filled fellow pastors who came around me following a family tragedy that almost took me out. They lovingly with care walked me out of my darkness and back into the light. I am forever grateful.

Earle is a leader and greatly gifted preacher of holiness who has inspired me over and over to rejoice in the message of optimistic grace that is our spiritual heritage. I love to hear the man preach.

116

Jo Anne and I arrived on the General Board of The Wesleyan Church at the same time. I cannot tell you how refreshing it was to me to hear this woman of God talk often and freely about the Holy Spirit. And to watch him work in her and through her. And then to get to have a front-row seat to watch the Lord anoint her for such astounding leadership in the church was a true joy.

Ernest came into my life when I needed a right-hand man in ministry. I found in him a profound faith that grew out of his rich life of prayer. The presence of the Lord shines out of his countenance and his unshakeable confidence in the readiness of the Lord to answer prayer gave me courage and strength I could not find in myself. And we laughed a lot together, too.

Kris, Matthew and Josh are our three boys. They love the Lord with all their hearts. They are not perfect but they are wonderful men of God. And they have audacious faith. Sometimes I want to say, "Gracious, boys, I know that's what I preached and tried to live out before you, but you're scaring me to death!" Shame on me and good for them.

Cynthia is my wife. I have been the agent of her sanctification, I'm afraid. She is the best person I have ever met in my life. Kerry Willis (now a Nazarene District Superintendent) was a little boy in Cynthia's home church on Harkers Island. When he heard she and I were getting married, he was mortified. He considered Cynthia to be right up there with the Virgin Mary! Sorry, Kerry. But you really weren't that far off. This precious girl has been Exhibit A to me and to every congregation we served that there is such a thing as an entirely sanctified life.

Then there's Mom. For most of their lives Mom was the only one of the six children of my godly grandparents who lived for the Lord. The others found their way into the kingdom – a couple of them by the skin of their teeth – but she has lived her whole life in surrender to God. Everyone who knows her dearly loves this 90 year old saint. And she loves them back. I believe if you were to unpile all the rocks piled on the Rock of Ages, right down there next to the Solid Rock upon whom the church is built, you would find a beautiful Little Rock with the name, Christyna (how appropriate) on it. Thanks, Mom, for loving me into the kingdom of our God and of his Christ!

Forget the arguments. Live the life. Share the testimony. Let the glory of the Lord shine out of your life unimpeded. Be a person of authenticity and integrity. Let your life of authenticity and integrity shine like the stars in this present darkness.

Let the River of Life flow from within you, pure and unpolluted, so that when thirsty people drink from your life they are not repulsed by your distasteful pride but refreshed by the Holy Spirit who abides in you. Let your life be accessible. In this matter, more is caught than taught. Be contagious. Live close enough to them that they catch what you've got. And be sure you have something worth catching.

Let your life be overflowing with Holy Love. When they squeeze you, ooze love. When they provoke you, speak love. When they mistreat you and say all manner of evil about you, respond in love. Let him who is Love have access to every space in your life. Let him leak out of you all over everyone who makes contact with you.

Live your life in such a way that puts you on the list when they ask those who know you, "Who most influenced you to pursue a life of holiness?"

Esse quam videri.

CHAPTER NINETEEN

HOLINESS REDICOVERED

How The Wesleyan Church Can Get Back
What We Gave Away

FOUR DIMENSIONAL DISCIPLESHIP

I believe the best delivery system for a rediscovery of our holiness heritage in The Wesleyan Church is through an intentional discipleship path that is focused on producing sanctified believers who are not content until they have made the enemy mad.

We have produced a bunch of excellent preachers and a bunch of good people in The Wesleyan Church. We have been especially good at building ministries for children and teens. That's one of our greatest accomplishments. We have built some strong local churches, including some phenomenal mega churches, way more than can be expected or explained for a denomination our size. We have developed excellent colleges and universities that love their direct connection to The Wesleyan Church and are a key to driving the mission of the Church. Some of our excellent professors are leaders in their field of studies, and strong proponents of the holiness message.

We have done a wonderful job of leading people to Christ, staying true to the Word, and guarding our founding principles, the Articles of Religion. We are led by godly leaders who love God and in whom we have the utmost confidence. We are invading enemy territory with anointed young church planters and exciting, wineskin-stretching church plants. And we are carrying this mission to new places all over the globe.

We have built a good, solid foundation for our recovery. And we have a receptive group of emerging young leaders who are hungry for holiness. And one of the unintended consequences of our slide into evangelicalism is, this new generation is not tainted by all the baggage that accumulated around us as the holiness movement rolled to a stop. They are a fresh, clean slate upon which the Holy Spirit can write a new story. A robust, holiness-oriented discipleship path can be laid out before The Wesleyan Church, and if we walk in that path, we can once again be a holiness church. Without the baggage.

When he was leading the Department of Spiritual Formation, Jim Dunn built a three-fold communication concept that gave the department direction for its mission. Everything they did was run through this cognitive grid: Head, Heart, Hands. After some experience and conversation outside the department, a fourth concept was added. Habits.

If the whole world went haywire and I was suddenly made the boss of The Wesleyan Church, here is what I would do.

The Leadership

I would galvanize the Leadership Team around this mission. My constant message to them would be: You have one job regardless of your specific assignment, and that is to drive the conversation in the Church using "Pathway" or "Journey" language, emphasizing the process of sanctification and talking about the importance of sanctification. Use the terms Head, Heart, Hands, Habits, to communicate this message. Bring people to the table who know what they are talking about, practitioners not theorists, and who have an experience worth sharing and a life above reproach.

Do not produce just a multiplicity of random programs, but produce Wesleyan material which will support the "Rediscovering Our Holiness Heritage" mission, using discipleship as the delivery system at all levels and in all areas of The Wesleyan Church.

Craft a short, memorable mission statement that is comprehensive, sharply focused, compelling, memorable and looks good on a t-shirt. Use college kids and young pastors to help you with this. Put sanctification in a prominent place in that statement. Keep it simple. Say it over and over until people are finishing your sentences for you. Burn it into our hearts.

Talk your head off. Run your legs off. Pray your heart out. Think until your brain explodes. At the end of eight years there should be nothing left in the tank.

Then I would build our entire ministry focus, top to bottom, on this Four Dimensional Discipleship model.

Head

We know this part well. We have done this part well. We know the value of and the process for sharing information with our people that grounds them in the Word of God. But in the rising generation, where there is now no Sunday school systematically teaching foundational truths, we find ourselves with a biblically impoverished people. This has to change. The Sunday school mission may have passed away from The Wesleyan Church but the discipleship mission has not, and never will. Whatever way we decide to do it, not doing it is not an option.

And just the sharing of facts with no direction or action following is not an option either. Let the days be gone when our expectation was to "learn" and "change", with no "do" in the equation. When I was a young church planter, a handful of us had the opportunity to spend some time with Floyd Schwanz, the Small Groups Pastor for New Hope Church in Portland, Oregon, led by Dale Galloway. Halfway through the conversation, he walked over to the whiteboard and drew a picture he called "the big-headed little kid". It was a stick figure with a tiny stick-figure body with a huge round head. This kid's head filled most of the whiteboard. He said, "This is discipleship in the North American church." He was right. We filled our heads with enough facts to save the world multiple times over, and our heads just grew bigger and bigger, but our skimpy little bodies got no exercise because we just sat there and did nothing with what we learned. Then he quoted John Maxwell, "We are educated far beyond the level of our obedience."

This One Dimensional Discipleship model will not bring revolution and revitalization in holiness to our Church. We need to faithfully engage the head, but we cannot stop there.

Heart

We must also engage the heart. This is where we draw our people closer to the heart of God. This is where we emphasize the importance of a personal experience, a personal encounter with the Living God of the Universe who wants to have an ongoing relationship with them. This is where we talk with them about sanctification.

This is actually our strongest point. The criticism we have for the Reformed theological orientation that is so prevalent in the North American church and is way over-represented in the Christian publishing field, is that it is long on information but too often fails to move to the experience, to the heart, to the transformation. In this post-modern culture, where we know more than anyone has ever known, young thinkers are searching more for meaning than for more information. They are tired of sterile facts. They are looking for answers for their lives. This message of sanctification is tailor-made for these young seekers.

Central to Wesley's discipleship path of the sanctified life was the honest and earnest examination of the heart, both by the believer and in a circle of believers. *The Band Meeting: Rediscovering Relational Discipleship in Transformational Community* by Kevin Watson and Scott Kisker from *seedbed* (the publishing arm of Asbury Theological Seminary) and Jon Wiest's book, *Banding Together: A Practical Guide for Disciple Makers* both attempt to recover the intense and intentional community-centered dynamic of discipleship that North American Christianity has neglected and abandoned in favor of the classroom dissemination of Bible facts. The focus of banded discipleship is on the heart, which we all know in its fallen state is deceitful above all things, and desperately wicked. It definitely needs a cure that head-knowledge alone will not provide.

Like Watson, Kisker and Wiest, our best thinkers need to be writing books and blogs and articles about the sanctified life. They do not need to be emotionally based. But they do need to engage the emotions along with the mind. And a thoughtful, heartfelt presentation of this deeper life will strike a fire in the hearts of this generation, kindling a desire to know more about this dynamic relationship of holy love.

When John Wesley said, "There is no holiness apart from social holiness," he was not making a statement primarily about social justice, as some think. He was really talking about there being no such thing as isolated discipleship. We are meant to follow Christ together, in fellowship, loving one another, bearing the burdens of one another and encouraging one another. This generation finds itself increasingly isolated and is hungry for deep and meaningful, trustworthy fellowship. They will be drawn to the authentic fellowship of sanctified believers reaching out to them in a spirit of Holy Love.

One of the basic tenets of communication is, "Keep it simple. Say it often. Make it burn." It is attributed to a number of people, including at least one scoundrel, but it is true to effective communication. It needs to be true of us as our brightest and best are recruited to share this heart-impacting message in a compelling way with the insulated in the church and the isolated in the rest of the world. We need to set their hearts on fire.

Hands

Here is where our previous efforts in discipleship too often fell short. We did nothing much with all we knew. We thought it was about us and making us better and better Christians. So we just kept getting better and better and better and better. That is human nature. Whatever it is we engage in or endeavor to accomplish, it comes to us and it stops with us. It's kind of like the Dead Sea. It's dead because, as one of the lowest places on the face of the earth, everything flows in but nothing flows out. And it smells bad, too, if you've ever been there. That is not the way it is with the kingdom of God. We are not ponds. We are rivers. We are not containers. We are conduits. And grace flows from what is in our heads and our hearts, out through our hands.

Evangelism and compassion are the two most common ways God uses our hands in his work.

A spirit of evangelism without judgment now resides in The Wesleyan Church. We are definitely an open-armed people. It was not always so with us. We were so guarded and protective of the holiness doctrine, people seeking the Lord often found it difficult to get around us to get to him. I am reminded of the Southern Gospel singer, Howard Goodman, who came up through the same kind of strictness in the Pentecostal church. He was asked near the end of his life, if he had it to do over again, what would he change? This precious man said, "I'd let more people into heaven." I think we get that part. We let God man the gate. We understand it's our job to fill the line.

The other part we are getting right more often is engaging our hands in compassionate ministries. Our younger generation is pro-active in this. They are much more like their great grandparents than they are like their parents. We are remodeling rundown houses and replacing leaking roofs in the name of Jesus. We are building ramps and porches for poor widows in the name of Jesus. We are filling backpacks and feeding hungry children in the name of Jesus. We are filling semi-truck trailers and airplanes with supplies for people who have been brutalized by natural disasters. We are breaking addictions and building wells in the name of Jesus. We are tearing down walls and working for racial healing in the name of Jesus.

What Jo Anne Lyon has done with and through World Hope is unusual for her (my) generation. We are the couch potato generation. But the rising generation in our Church, inspired by her, has grabbed hold of the fight for clean water, the fight against human trafficking, the fight for peace in war-torn places, and the fight for medical intervention in the face of epidemic. World Hope is who we should have been all the time. In fact, I wonder if it is too much to say that every local Wesleyan church should look a little bit like World Hope or The Salvation Army, without the red kettles. "Blood and Fire". Saved, sanctified and serving. That's who the Wesleys were, and if we are going to bear their name, shouldn't we be more like them?

Habits

This sounds like human effort to old Wesleyans. Or something we should be breaking, not embracing. But the truth is, God made us to be habitual people. It's the fall that twisted that into something bad.

In their book, *Awakening Grace: Spiritual Practices to Transform Your Soul*, a book about the practical implications of the world's most impractical idea, Matt LeRoy and Jeremy Summers turn the concept of Christian discipline inside out when they say, "We easily fall into thinking that the work of spiritual formation rests on us. That it is our duty to master the disciplines of Bible reading, justice, prayer and service. But these practices are not the focus. God is. These practices are pathways that lead us to him. These disciplines are not the end but the means of grace."

They go on to offer a new perspective, a shift, in how we perceive spiritual disciplines, by placing the emphasis on God's grace at work in the practice instead of on our performance of the action. It's a shift from mastery of a discipline to submission to grace, a shift from practice as a tool for growth to practice as a teacher of the soul, a shift from growth through certain formulas to discipleship as unpredictable journey.

Their message is that spiritual disciplines – the habits of holiness – have little lasting effect if imposed from the outside in. In fact, they do just the opposite of what we intend and need. They have a corrosive effect on our spiritual life. We have clearly established, both in our knowledge of scripture and our own sad experience of "striving for holiness", that this outside-in effort is legalism and legalism kills the soul. It does not bring us to life. It is our surrender to God the Holy Spirit in day-by-day, moment-by-moment obedience that brings life to our souls, fits us for heaven, makes us a blessing here, and is a good habit for us to practice.

Head. Heart. Hands. Habit. I sincerely believe, if God would so choose to be in it, a discipleship model based on this plan, intentionally, enthusiastically, and with God-given anointing employed throughout The Wesleyan Church, would produce a fully engaged people, fully surrendered to God in every area of their lives, intent on fully interfering with the godless agenda of the world, and fully committed to bringing to pass God's grand redemptive plan for the world.

That's a whole lot of optimism right there. But we're optimistic people. So that's what I'd do if they put me in charge. But no one needs to make me the boss of anything. God has raised up among us wonderful, Spirit-filled leaders whose hearts are fully committed to him. If what I am saying is from God, then it already resides in their hearts and minds as well. They will take us there. And I'm ready to go there with them.

PART FOUR

HOLINESS EXPERIENCED

How We Can Lead Our People into the
Deeper Grace of the Sanctified Life

"Preach faith till you have it; and then because you have it,
you will preach faith."

Peter Bohler to John Wesley

CHAPTER TWENTY

HOLINESS EXPERIENCED

How We Can Lead Our People into the Deeper Grace of the Sanctified Life

THE SANCTIFIED LIFE IS LIFE IN THE SPIRIT

Romans 8:1-39

There is a life to which every human aspires. It will look different according to that person's culture, circumstances, upbringing, aptitude or imagination, but it will be there. It is a life of abundance, fulfillment and joy. It is innate in every person. It is in there because God put it there. In the book of wisdom, Ecclesiastes 3:11, we are told that he has put eternity in our hearts. However we might define that, God defines it as life in the Spirit.

John Wesley draws for us an engaging word picture describing the two choices available to the child of God: life in the flesh or life in the Spirit.

> From long experience and observation, I am inclined to think that whoever finds redemption in the blood of Jesus, whoever is justified, has then the choice of walking in the higher or the lower path. I believe the Holy Spirit at that time sets before him the "more excellent way," and incites him to walk therein; to choose the narrowest path in the narrow way; to aspire after the heights and depths of holiness – after the entire image of God. But if he does not accept this offer, he insensibly declines into the lower order of Christians. He still goes on in what may be called a good way, serving God in his degree, and finds mercy in the close of life, through the blood of the covenant. (*Sermon 89: "The More Excellent Way"*)

Like a friend once said to me, "We like to take John Wesley's sermons and improve on them," so I am going to be bold enough to add this observation from my much more limited knowledge and experience. I believe that along the lower path, our Loving God draws close to the struggling believer, puts his arm around his or her shoulder during the time of trial or temptation that comes from walking that more perilous path, and whispers, "There is a better way. If you will trust me, I would love to show it to you and walk there with you." And this happens, I believe, all along the lower way.

That is life in the Spirit, embraced by the love of God.

Let's walk through Romans 8 together exploring life in the Spirit in the context of the love of God for us and his entire creation. The reality of our existence is, we live in a fallen world, and the central message of Romans 8 is that there is a life filled with love – life in the Spirit – which begins with "no condemnation" and ends with "no separation". We have a Loving God who is deeply invested in us, will not abandon us and is not predisposed to condemn us. He is predisposed to love us. And that never changes.

As we sing, in the words of Caleb Culver, Cory Asbury and Ran Jackson, "It chases me down, fights 'til I'm found."

> "There's no shadow you won't light up,
> Mountain you won't climb up, Coming after me.
> There's no wall you won't kick down,
> Lie you won't tear down, Coming after me."

That is life in the Spirit, pursued by the love of God.

Life in the Spirit is a life of optimistic grace, and those who are in Christ Jesus have discovered the wonderful truth that the law of the Spirit of life sets us free from the law of sin and death. Life under the Law, in contrast, is a life that is powerless because we cannot keep the obligations of the Law due to the weakness of our flesh, our sinful nature. The Law can condemn us before God, and it can separate us from God. It cannot love us to God or give us life in God. Only the Spirit of God can do that.

That is life in the Spirit, freed from condemnation by the love of God.

Paul stresses that only God has the power to overcome the downward pull of our sinful nature and compensate for the weakness of our flesh. The Calvary event secured this promise in reality for us – the death of Christ on the cross for the forgiveness of our sins, and the power of his resurrection to raise us to new life in him. "He breaks the power of cancelled sin (our justification) and sets the prisoner free (our sanctification)," we learn from Charles Wesley. "If we confess our sins, he is faithful and just and will forgive us our sins (our justification) and purify us from all unrighteousness (our sanctification)," we learn from the Apostle John. "Be of sin the double cure: Save from wrath (our justification) and make us pure (our sanctification)," we learn from Augustus M. Toplady, an Anglican with Calvinist leanings and an outspoken opponent of the Wesleys, who in spite of himself confirmed their cardinal doctrine. Justified and sanctified.

That is life in the Spirit, purified in our hearts by the love of God.

Paul is bold to assert that God condemns sin. He does not condemn us. He condemned sin through the death of Christ on the cross, and his resurrection in righteousness is both imputed to us (counted as righteousness in our behalf – our justification) and imparted to us (making us righteous in our character through the purifying power of his Holy Spirit residing and reigning in us – our sanctification). Through him we meet the righteous requirements of the Law as he empowers us to live according to the direction of the Spirit, not the impulse of the sinful nature.

That is life in the Spirit, empowered by the love of God.

Paul helps us understand our reality. This is literally a matter of life and death for us. The things of the Spirit are even more real than the things of this life in the flesh. Just because we cannot see them does not mean they are not real. When we, by the help of the Holy Spirit, begin to see things as God sees them, our mindset changes.

If our minds are focused on the life of this world, that orientation will put us on a downward path away from God and straight into the gravitational pull of death – impacting us in a negative way physically, spiritually, eternally. Minds that are focused on the life in the Spirit find an infilling of life and peace – impacting us in a positive way physically, spiritually, eternally. A mind dominated by a spirit of selfish desire produces a spirit that is hostile to God, because the sinful nature and the Spirit of God are put into competition with each other. It cannot help itself. And it cannot please God.

A person who submits to the control of the Spirit of God has an entirely different experience than that. That person experiences freedom, as strange as that may sound when we are talking about being under another's control. But we are not talking about being under just anyone's control. We are talking about being under the control of the personal presence of our God, himself, who loves us and, in Christ, gave himself for us.

That is life in the Spirit, surrendered to the love of God.

The person living in the Spirit also experiences the joy of belonging. Paul proclaims that those who are led by the Spirit are the children of God. We are adopted into his family and he works in us to build the family traits in us, so that anyone who meets us recognizes, "Oh, he looks like his Father!" Or, "Oh, she resembles her brothers and sisters." Jonathan David Helser, Brian Joel Case and Mark Johnson teach us to sing, echoing the spirit of John Wesley and his heartwarming experience at Aldersgate, "I'm no longer a slave to fear. I am a child of God." And the Spirit himself continues to whisper this fact in our ear. It's called "the witness of the Spirit", one of the major theological contributions John Wesley and the Methodists made to their and our generation – the recovery of this wonderful gift from God to his children, that we can know we belong to him.

That is life in the Spirit, living in the assurance of the love of God.

Wesleyan thought leaders Steve DeNeff and David Drury authored *Soul Shift: The Measure of a Life Transformed*. It is a beautiful expression of discipleship in the Wesleyan understanding of the sanctification process, a pathway of growth in grace that leads to life transformation. It is all about transformation, not about outward behavior modification. DeNeff and

Drury build their system on seven concept couplets that measure the movement in a person's life from self-centeredness to Christlikeness: Me to You, Slave to Child, Seen to Unseen, Consumer to Steward, Ask to Listen, Sheep to Shepherd, and Me to We. The key shift in the entire process is Slave to Child. If this one does not take place, the others do not take place. It is this dynamic, from Romans 8:15, that drives the rest of the process. Who are we in Christ? Who does our Heavenly Father, our Creator and Redeemer, say we are? "For you did not receive a spirit that makes you a slave again to fear, but you received the Spirit of sonship. And by him we cry, '*Abba,*Father'."

That is life in the Spirit, transformed from being a slave again to fear into being a child of God through the dynamic power of the love of God.

Slavery is death. It is the Spirit that gives us life. If we do not have the Spirit of the Living God living within us, and giving us this life, we do not belong to Christ. Not to be morbid, but he does not have any dead children. His children live forever in the power of Christ's resurrection. And this life now and forevermore is lived in a spirit of life and peace. And we do not live this life as orphans. We have a Heavenly Father who loves us and claims us as his own. We know him in a close up and personal way. An "Abba Father" kind of way.

The term, Abba, appears three times in scripture. Jesus prays to "Abba Father" in Mark 14:36, pleading for release or resolve. In Galatians 4:6, Paul says it is the Spirit in us who cries out, "Abba Father", because we are the children of God. Here in Romans 8, Paul says, again, it is by the Spirit that we call out, "Abba Father", because he testifies alongside our spirit that we are the children of God. It is the defining, intimate term in Aramaic for the father a child knows well and has a personal relationship with. There were more formal names for a father in the languages of the day. This was not one of those formal terms. This is a "Daddy" kind of term.

In excruciating agony, Jesus calls upon his Father. In exhilarating joy, along with Paul we call upon our Father. In every emotion and condition in between, those who know God in a personal way call upon him in a personal way. It is the Spirit who prompts us and teaches us to do that. If we belong to Christ, which we do by his grace, we share in his sufferings and we share in his glory. And we share in his relationship with Abba Father.

That is life in the Spirit, being adopted into the family by the love of God.

Being part of a family includes standing in there when the times get tough. We do not share just in the glory of being children of God, but we also have to take our beatings for being part of his family. Later in Romans 8, Paul is going to refer to this: "He who did not spare his own Son, but gave him up for us all" is balanced by the all too accurate description of life in the Spirit that recognizes,

> "For your sake we face death all day long; we are considered as sheep to be slaughtered."

There is a reality to life in the Spirit that includes opposition, persecution and nasty treatment from people who do not know the love of God in a personal way. If Jesus was not exempt, we are not exempt. It is true that God will draw a line in our lives that evil cannot cross, but it is also true that he seems to draw that line deeper into our lives than we would prefer. It is true that he will bear our burdens. It is not true that he will not give us more than we can bear. It is true that he will not give us more than he can bear.

That is life in the Spirit, bearing the reproach and shame of Christ for the joy set before us in the love of God.

To another group of people, and to us, Paul said that no trial or test would come to us that was not common to us all, and that God is faithful – he will not let us be tested or tried beyond what we can bear, but will always provide a way out so that we can pass the test. As we read Romans 8, we come to understand that all of creation is experiencing this test, and is groaning under the weight of it. The only thing that keeps us going is the hope we have in a good God who is at work in our world, setting the limits on evil, and bringing it ever closer to its full redemption.

That is life in the Spirit, hoping patiently for the certainty of the full expression of the love of God in this fallen world.

Does it encourage you that in this passage we are told that the Spirit of God himself, dwelling within us, is interceding to the Loving Father for us? And then we learn that Christ himself is at the right hand of God and is also interceding for us. Even when we do not know how to put the right words together for a sensible prayer, he who searches our hearts and knows the mind of the Spirit intercedes for us in accordance with God's will.

Wait a minute. Do you mean to tell me that God himself is reading the mind of God himself and is praying for me to God himself according the express will of God himself? What do you think the odds are of that prayer being answered by our loving God himself?

That is life in the Spirit, praying in full confidence that I am encapsulated in the love of God.

In a messed up world, where we know we are exposed to the devices of the enemy on the one hand, and we know we are not shielded from the sad realities of the fallen world on the other hand, there is a good God involved in the circumstances of our lives. As a good Wesleyan, I know that everything that happens to me is not God's express will for my life. Many things fall within his permissive will that he does not necessarily choose directly for me. But our good God is so great that he can take the worst thing that could ever happen and turn it into the greatest event of history. That's what the cross is all about. If he can do that, then he can handle anything I am asked to face. And he will, for my good and for his glory. He has pre-determined from the very beginning that these things would work to make me become over time conformed to the likeness of his Son. It is my process of sanctification.

That is life in the Spirit, growing to be like Christ through the love of God.

Taking all of this into account – my sinful nature redeemed by Christ, my hostility toward God replaced by life and peace, my dead spirit brought to life through the power of Christ's resurrection, my slave chains broken by the mercy of God, my alienation replaced by my adoption into his family, my bondage to decay broken by his glorious freedom, my pain alleviated by his hope and healing, my groaning completely understood by his divine knowledge, my troubles swallowed up in his power – what should we say?

Who in hell below or heaven above could possibly mount an effective attack against the irrepressible, unconquerable love of God for us?

Who or what can separate me from this love? Trouble? No. Hardship? No. Persecution? It tried but couldn't. Famine? Nakedness? Sword? No, no, and no. Either death or life? No. Angels or demons? Angels wouldn't, demons would but can't. Things now? No. Things out there in the future? I don't know what's out there, but I know who's out there, so, no. Any powers? None. Height? No. Depth? No. Anything at all – in all of creation? Nothing. Nothing can separate us from the love of God that is in Christ Jesus our Lord.

That is life in the Spirit, living as more than a conqueror through the love of God.

Let's be honest. I know I can mess up my relationship with God, and I can even walk away from that relationship. But no matter what I do, he will always love me. He will always seek me. He will always pursue me. He will always watch for me to come home. He will always call after me. He will always love me. So why would I walk away? I want to love him as much as he loves me. And I want to love others the same way he loves them. Like a little boy with his daddy, I want to be just like my Heavenly Father.

God loves us so much that he invested the life and death and life of his Son (to borrow a phrase) in us, and stays constantly in touch with us by placing his personal presence, the Holy Spirit, within us, so he could impact the rest of the world he loves through us.

Living in the love of God. Living with the love of God in us. Living life as life was meant to be lived. That is life in the Spirit.

CHAPTER TWENTY-ONE

HOLINESS EXPERIENCED

How We Can Lead Our People into the
Deeper Grace of the Sanctified Life

THE SANCTIFIED LIFE IS LIFE DRAWN FROM THE VINE

John 15:1-17

You know about kudzu, right? Kudzu was first introduced from the Pacific to North America in 1876, at the Japanese Pavilion at the Centennial Exposition in Philadelphia. It made its major introduction in the 1930s, planted by the government in the southeastern United States as an agent of erosion control.

Kudzu is a leafy vine that grows at an astounding rate and takes over an area at the rate of 2,500 acres a year. It is a competitive plant that coils and climbs and covers everything. It is not a parasite, but it does kill the trees and other vegetation in the area it occupies. It does that by out-competing the other plants for life resources, especially sunlight. As it covers a tree, its broad leafs block the sunlight from reaching the host tree, eventually leading to the demise of the tree. It does the same to the ground cover around it. During its peak growing season, you can actually measure its growth overnight. Amazing.

The sad thing about kudzu is that it has little value to offer as a food source for animals, or for its medicinal qualities, or for utilitarian use. It grows rapidly and is healthy, but it gives back next to nothing. It takes life. It chokes out life. If plants have attitudes, this one is completely self-absorbed.

It is an apt illustration of life lived for itself, unconnected to the source of true Life, abundant life, Jesus Christ. There is a better way.

The Apostle John, in his account of the gospel, dedicated chapters 13 through 17 to the final last words of Jesus before his death on the cross. Famous last words are important words, and John draws from his memory and the aid of the Holy Spirit to wring out the very last drop of wisdom and direction from the Lord. Among the word pictures Jesus used on that night in the Upper Room is the picture of the life-giving vine.

Vineyards were common in his day in his setting. And they were generally well-cared for, because the fruit of the vine was so essential to life in that arid land. Jesus drew a picture of a healthy, growing vine, drawing its life from the soil, being cared for by the Master Gardener and growing in its ability to bear fruit.

The vine imagery was no stranger to his hearers. Their prophets had used this imagery over and over in their messages to the Jewish people. The prophets, however, generally used the image of the vine in a negative way – something bearing great promise but producing great disappointment. Isaiah 5:1-2 reads,

> I will sing to the one I love a song about his vineyard:
> My loved one had a vineyard on a fertile hillside.
> He dug it up and cleared it of stones and
> planted it with the choicest vines.
> He built a watchtower in it and cut out a winepress as well.
> Then he looked for a crop of good grapes,
> but it yielded only bad fruit.

In John 15, Jesus is intent on helping his disciples, them and us, understand that there is a brighter picture, a way of hope, a True Vine that bears good fruit abundantly. In this chapter he speaks of this True Vine having branches, and the fruit is borne on those branches, and the fruit is described as fruit, more fruit, much fruit, and fruit that will last. This is a picture of spiritual growth, growth in grace and character, in the life of the believer. It is a picture of the sanctified life.

In the word picture of Jesus, in order for this growth to happen, there are two conditions that must be met. First, the bearing branches must remain in healthy connection to the life-giving vine. Break the connection, the branch dies, there is no fruit. Second, the branches must undergo purposeful and necessary pruning. No pruning, the life of the vine is directed into growing more bigger and better branches. With proper pruning, the life of the vine is directed into growing more bigger and better fruit.

The sanctified life is an abundant life that comes from the Lord of Life, Jesus Christ. There are many other potential sources that appear to offer life, but true life comes only through the True Vine. People try vainly to fill their lives with an abundance of possessions, but there is no Life there. Relationships that seem to be so full of promise too often end in disappointment if we are deceived into believing they will be a source of life for us – there is no Life there. A friend of mine told me recently that he is making more money than he could have ever imagined, "But I hate my job." He can't wait until he retires and can do "something meaningful" with his life and his money. (I'm a preacher so I made a couple of suggestions!) Piles of possessions, positions of prominence, places of importance. These are dead ends, not sources of Life. The endless efforts to disguise our aging and present a cosmetically altered appearance is a vain effort to pursue our infatuation with youthfulness. There is no Life there, only paint. If the barn needs paint, paint it, but it's still just an old barn. Anything that presents itself as a substitute for Real Life is only a substitute, not the real thing. There is no Life there. But a life being sanctified by the flowing stream of vitality coming to us through the True Vine brings Life eternal, abundant and full. The process of sanctification takes place as we live in connection to the True Vine, just as the life of the grape vine flows through the branches in a healthy process of bringing in nutrients and carrying away waste. The Life is in the Vine.

The sanctified life is an unimpeded, healthy life, as the Life from the True Vine is allowed to flow freely through us. I am not a vine master. I know nothing about growing grapes, first hand. But I know human life. So I assume that in the life of a grapevine, there must be certain things that impede health and growth. I imagine bugs and certain worms would be a problem. Soil content that puts too much or too little of certain nutrients into the vine would have to be accounted for, I would imagine. Disease would impair vine health and impact fruit production. Birds that love grapes would be a nuisance. I know firsthand in Life in the Spirit, there are any number of influences that can and will impede spiritual growth. Paul spoke to the heart of the matter when he compared our attitudes with that of Christ Jesus, in Philippians 2, and admonished those who were being sanctified, "Do nothing out of selfish ambition or vain conceit, but in humility consider others better than yourselves. Each of you should look not only to your own interests, but also to the interests of others. Your attitude should be the same as that of Christ Jesus." Selfish ambition, vanity, conceit, pride, competition, comparison, self-interest would all be impediments to the flow of the Life from the True Vine, and to the ongoing work of the Spirit who desires to make us like Christ.

The sanctified life is a carefully attended life. If you read on in Isaiah 5, you see a picture of an untended grapevine. "I will take away its hedge, and it will be destroyed. I will break down its wall, and it will be trampled. I will make it a wasteland, neither pruned nor cultivated, and briers and thorns will grow there." That is the picture of the untended life, and God's merciful withholding of blessing in order to bring that life to repentance and True Life. He loves us too much to let us be deceived into believing our untended life is an abundant life. To the contrary, the tended life, the life cared for by the Master Gardener, God the Farmer, is protected, nourished, pruned and cultivated, so that it will produce an ample harvest of fruit. As much as we may not enjoy the pruning, we certainly enjoy the fruit it produces, and we certainly enjoy it more than the devastation that would come to us without his loving involvement in our life. He is careful to care for us. In turn, we should be careful to live a careful life.

The sanctified life is a fruitful life. Imagine you are standing among the Israelite nation, waiting for the return of the final two spies who were among the twelve sent to reconnoiter the land of Canaan. You stretch your neck to see, hoping they bring a better report than the others. Off in the distance you see them, but they seem to be struggling to make progress. As they move closer, you realize why. Between them, they are carrying a pole on their shoulders and it is sagging. It is sagging because they have loaded it down with some poor guy's grapevine – and it is so full of grapes they can hardly carry it. And bunches of grapes are dragging the ground. That is the life God desires for you. He desires to pour out his blessings in your life in such a way that it is almost more than you can carry. And certainly more than you yourself can – or should – consume. That is the sanctified life of abundant fruit he desires to produce in and through you.

Too many times, we holiness folk have been content to stop right here and rejoice in all that God has done for us – and we forget why. It's not about us. It's about those who are not yet connected to the True Vine, those whose lives are dried up, barren and dead. It's about us reaching them for Christ and the kingdom. The sanctified life is a sacramental life. Those grapes must be crushed to bring life and refreshment to others. He who is the True Vine is also the poured out wine of sacrifice, a sacrament of salvation for all who will "drink of this cup." I do not know if grapevines feel pain or remorse – the pain of the ripping away of the bunch of grapes from the branch, or the remorse of the loss of what the branch labored to produce. But your sanctified life is going to be painful for you. There is no salvation apart from sacrifice. There is no sanctification apart from pain. Paul, again, this time in Philippians 3:10-11, had it right when he acknowledged, "I want to know Christ and the power of his resurrection and the fellowship of sharing in his sufferings, becoming like him in his death, and so, somehow, to attain to the resurrection from the dead." That is what being connected to the True Vine leads us to – life in Christ, and a death to ourselves, that leads to a Christlike life. That is the sanctified life.

It is no accident that the Department of Tourism in Israel uses the image of Joshua and Caleb carrying that swaying pole holding that abundant harvest of grapes as their image for what awaits those who visit their land. There is no reason why that image should not also represent our lives in Christ, as we walk through a barren and desert land and say to those we meet, "I have come from a place you have not yet been. I have seen things you have not yet seen. I have something for you, here, that you just have to try. Believe me, you're going to love it."

And what is that fruit? According to Jesus, in John 15:9-14, it is nothing other than love.

"As the Father has loved me, so I have loved you. Now remain in my love. If you obey my commands, you will remain in my love, just as I have obeyed my Father's commands and remain in his love. I have told you this so that my joy may be in you and that your joy may be complete. My command is this: Love each other as I have loved you. Greater love has no one than this, that one lay down his life for his friends. You are my friends if you do what I command."

In verses 16 and 17, he drives home the point of how important it is that we bear this identifying fruit of love in our lives. It is the key to our effectiveness in ministry through the favor of God on our lives. Again, not for us, but for others.

"You did not choose me, but I chose you to go and bear fruit – fruit that will last. Then the Father will give you whatever you ask in my name. This is my command: Love each other."

Who is included in "each other"? People like us who like us? Our own each other? Not if Jesus was right when he said, "You have heard that it was said, 'Love your neighbor and hate your enemy.' But I tell you, love your enemies and pray for those who persecute you" (Matthew 5:43-44). It's all the "each others". He also said, "By this everyone will know you are my disciples, if you love one another" (John 13:35). That would be, again, all the "one anothers".

The Apostle Paul recognized the prominence of love as the fruit of a life drawn from the Vine in his list of the nine dimensions of loving relationships, what he termed "the fruit of the Spirit". This fruit is the character of Christ emerging through the sanctifying power of the Holy Spirit at work in the life of the growing believer. Those who live by the flesh demonstrate the sinful, harmful, relationship-killing actions of the flesh. "But the fruit of the Spirit is love, joy, peace, patience, kindness, goodness, faithfulness, gentleness and self-control" (Galatians 5:22-23a). You do not have to be a seasoned follower of Christ to understand the circumstances and relationships that put this fruit to the test – those times that require gentleness or patience or faithfulness or self-control.

Our spiritual grandfather, John Wesley, the Grand Old Man of our theological heritage, was a man with an extraordinary ability to understand scripture and to communicate its meaning to others. And he was so able to keep things true to real life. Throughout the course of his ministry life he remained focused on one central truth: It is all about God's love filling us and expelling everything from us that is not love, and spilling over into the lives of those around us. In every circumstance and life experience.

Did he ever share that truth more eloquently than through this proclamation found in *A Plain Account of Christian Perfection*? In advising his Methodists not to seek gifts or glory, this blessing or that, Wesley said:

> It were well you should be thoroughly sensible of this: the heaven of heavens is love. There is nothing higher in religion: there is, in effect, nothing else. If you look for anything but more love, you are looking wide of the mark, you are getting out of the royal way, and when you are asking others, "have you received this or that blessing?", if you mean anything but more love, you mean wrong.

That life of love is the sanctified life, the life that draws its life from the True Vine, resembles the character of the True Vine, and bears the fruit the True Vine produces – the fruit of love, more love, much love, love that will last.

If you are seeking anything other than more love, you have missed the whole point.

CHAPTER TWENTY-TWO

HOLINESS EXPERIENCED

How We Can Lead Our People into the
Deeper Grace of the Sanctified Life

THE SANCTIFIED LIFE IS A LIFE OF OBEDIENCE

Learning to Say "Yes" to God
2 Corinthians 1:18-22

Every defining moment of my life has been marked by one thing:
It happened when I said "yes."

I was eight years old. My parents were singing in a youth revival in a
Nazarene Church in New Brighton, Pennsylvania. God broke in. The altar
was lined with young people seeking God. My mom came back to where I
and my baby sister were sitting. She noticed a tear rolling down my cheek.
She said, "Honey, is God speaking to you? Would you like to pray?" We
went forward and knelt at the front pew, Mom on one side and Dad on the
other. And I said, "Yes." The worst thing I had ever done was tell my
second grade neighbor there wasn't any Santa Claus! But that night I
became aware that I needed a Savior and I found one in Jesus. He drew me
to himself and that moment defined the direction, the quality and the
course of my life from that point forward.

By the way, it is as much a miracle to be saved from sin as it is to be saved
out of sin.

I already told about the Sunday night when I was eleven years old and
Sister Kiser asked me, "Do you want to be sanctified?" I could not have
defined for you, theologically, what happened to me that night. But

whatever it was, my heart-broken "no" when the pastor asked me if I got satisfied had been turned into a big old "yes" before it was all over, and whatever it was that God had for me in that moment, I had it.

I was fourteen years old. My dad was the evangelist for a revival meeting in New Boston, Ohio. I had actually gone to the altar a couple of times in that meeting. I couldn't figure out what God was dealing with me about. When you're fourteen, you have enough issues for God to deal with! When I went forward the third time, the folks probably thought dad had brought his own seeker. Maybe he was paying me to make him look good. As I prayed, we did not seem to be getting anywhere. Everybody else finally gave up but dad, and our friend Ray, who was playing the organ softly as we prayed. Finally, Ray stopped, slid off the organ bench and knelt beside me with his arm over my shoulder. I'll never forget his words whispered into my left ear: "Danny, is God calling you to preach?" Noooo. That can't be it. Then he said, "Just say 'Yes' from the bottom of your heart." I've always been a very visual person. When he said that, I pictured the bucket at my grandpa's old well. We weren't supposed to do this, but we always loved to just throw that bucket down the well. The rope would unwind, the crank would be flying in a circle, and that bucket would hit the water way down there. We'd watch, because when it hit, the reflection of the sky on the water would explode into a million pieces. I could see that "yes" tumbling to the bottom of my heart, and when it hit, God's Spirit witnessed to my spirit that, yes, he was calling me to preach.

The "yes" factor has been there in every one of those defining moments, and every one that has followed, and will be there in every one that is yet to come for me. If there was one secret I could impress upon our people that would totally transform their lives, it would be this (and I am ashamed to confess, I've learned it as much by painful neglect, as I have by faithful obedience): learn to say "yes" to God.

In 2 Corinthians 1:20, Paul says, "For no matter how many promises God has made, they are 'yes' in Christ." Too many times a relationship with God is seen as a list of prohibitions. Take the Ten Commandments, for example:

No other gods
No idols

No cussing
No buying on Sunday
No disrespect to parents
No stealing
No lying
No killing
No sex until you're married
No wanting other people's stuff

When we read this list, all we tend to hear is, "No. No. No. No. No. No. No. No. No. No." We don't hear the "yes" in all of that.

We don't hear . . .

If you will trust me, I will teach you how you can have a life-changing relationship with the very Living Creator of the universe.

If you will trust me, I will teach you how to love the Living God who will love you back.

If you will trust me, I will teach you how talk to each other in an uplifting, godly way.

If you will trust me, I will teach you how to learn to slow down and not put yourself at the center of life.

If you will trust me, I will teach you how to have an enriching relationship with the important people in your life, which will also teach you how to have that kind of relationship with me. (You'll learn who I am from your mom and dad, and you'll probably treat me like you treat them.)

If you will trust me, I will teach you how to value people above things.

If you will trust me, I will teach you how to be pure in heart and word, so people will see me in you, and they will know they can trust me because they know they can trust you.

If you will trust me, I will teach you how to respect life that is so precious to me that I would give my Son to redeem it.

If you will trust me, I will teach you how to be trustworthy in your relationships, and value that special bond I have created between you and the person I made you for. You'll learn how much I love you and how committed I am to you through that kind of love.

And, if you will trust me, I will teach you how to be satisfied, so you don't have to have everything everyone else has.

Those are not "no's". Those are all "yes's"! My friend, John Sutherland Logan, a great Scottish preacher, used to say that his mother taught him, "When God says 'no', he's saying 'yes' to greater things." Paul's principle is, learn to trust God so you can learn to say "yes" to him. There are at least three reasons I can think of why I can do that.

The first one is,
I can say "yes" to God because he has always said "yes" to me.

The foundation of our faith is expressed in the phrase Paul uses in this message to the Corinthian church, "as surely as God is faithful." The faithfulness of God is the bedrock upon which our faith is built. Hudson Taylor was a missionary to China who demonstrated great faith in his bold trust in the faithfulness of God. That was his definition of faith, coming out of his long and fruitful experience. "Faith is simply trusting in the faithfulness of God." His understanding, confirmed by God's faithfulness to him, is reflected in this great statement, "God's work done in God's way will never lack God's supply." Why? Because God is faithful. You can trust him.

The message of God to us, in Christ, is not a list of killjoy rules. It is not like a secret formula. If I can discover it and follow it, and put it all together just right, good things will happen to me! It is not "yes" this and "no" that, like a checklist. If I can just follow it, and not mess up, I can produce righteousness in my life. No. The message of the Gospel is Christ. He came to live among us to show us what God is like. He is the "Word of God", God's expression of himself. What you see in Jesus is exactly what God is like. And in Christ, God has always said, and is always saying, and will always say, "YES" to you and me.

146

Look at Romans 5:8. "God demonstrated his love for us in this way: while we were yet sinners, Christ died for us." While I was shaking my fist in his face, while I was spitting on the ground in contempt at the mention of his name, while I was running away from him as fast and as hard as my rebellion would take me, while I was screaming "no" at the top of my lungs, Christ was saying "yes" to me. Not after I turned around. Not after I cleaned myself up. Not after I made things right. Not after I apologized. While I was active in my sin — disobedient, hateful, selfish, mean, arrogant, lying, cheating, stealing, all-out sin — Christ said "yes", he would die for me to redeem me and live inside me by his Holy Spirit to make me holy. So I can say "yes" to a God like that, because he has always said "yes" to me.

A second reason I can say "yes" to God is because everything he has ever done for me has been good. Jesus Christ is the measure of God's attitude toward you and me. Listen to how Paul describes him:

> "Son" means that he holds a special position of privilege and authority. If you are not a parent, yet, you have a great day to look forward to when you will clearly understand how special your child is to you. And then you get to live that joy all over again when the grandchildren show up. Our children are special to us.

> And he is not just anybody's son. Paul says he's the "Son of God". That means he is unique, the only one. And he is divine. He holds every attribute of God Almighty.

> And he has a name. It's the name the angel told Joseph to give him: "Jesus, because he will save his people from their sins." He is the Savior of the world.

> And he has a title, "Christ". Why? Because he alone is the anointed One, he alone is the chosen One, he alone is the holy One. And he alone is good, and he represents everything God has ever done in my life, and it is always good.

In an earlier conversation with this church, Paul had said, "Jews demand miraculous signs and Greeks look for wisdom, but we preach Christ crucified: a stumbling block to Jews and foolishness to Gentiles, but to those whom God has called, both Jews and Greeks, Christ the power of God and the wisdom of God." And he is saying to them in this follow-up conversation (in so many words), "Do you know what, guys. We only have one message. It's not about making rules or breaking rules. It's not about impressing anybody. It's not about trying to impress God. When Silas, Timothy and I came to you, we had one message: the love of God given to you in his Son, the Lord Jesus Christ."

I can say "yes" to a God like that. I can trust a God like that. I can put my life in the hands of a God like that, because everything he has ever done for me has been good. Or as he told us and the church at Rome: "He who did not spare his own Son, but gave him up for us all — how will he not also, along with him, graciously give us all things?"

There's at least one more reason I can say "yes" to God.
That's because he loves to work out his good, perfect and pleasing will in my life.

His will for me is not "yes this" and "no that", but "yes always". What does that mean? When we were planting the church in Chapel Hill, one of our sons, as a high school student, was downtown on Franklin Street on Friday night. He walked up on a scene where a street preacher from The Lord's Church had been in a heated exchange with several college students. Street evangelism at its best. He arrived in time to hear one of the students say to the street preacher, "Why would I want to serve a God who is so hateful that he says he's going to throw me into hell if I don't serve him?" (If that were true, that would be a pretty good reason when you think about it.) But our son, seeing the opportunity to say a good word for Jesus said, "Wait, wait, wait, wait! Why wouldn't you want to serve a God who loves you so much he sent his Son to die on the cross in your place so you don't have to go to hell?"

That's not a "no". That's a big fat "yes" right there, if you're keeping score.

People don't like a vengeful, hateful "God" who is waiting to sweep us all into hell because of our disobedience. They say nasty things about that

"God". They don't like that "God" messing with what they're doing. They don't like being told "no". And we know that vengeful, hateful "God" can really get carried away. But, that is not the God of the Bible, our Heavenly Father who loved us so much he sent his Son to save us from our sins, and has taken up residence in our lives by his personal Presence, the Holy Spirit. When that God reveals his will and his way to us, we can actually say "yes" to him, because everything he does for us is designed to be good for us, not evil.

Now, as a good Wesleyan I understand that everything that happens to me isn't necessarily his first choice for me. What happens to me is all bound up in things I do, things other people do, things other people do to me, things I do to them, and the fact that I live in a broken world. Have you ever been hurt by someone and wondered where God was? Have you ever been hurt in church? Have you ever been hurt by church people? Were you tempted to blame God for that? God didn't do that to you. People did that to you.

It is absolutely true that nothing comes to me that does not first pass through his hands, so he has a say in it all. But it is also true that he always sets the limits on evil. He draws a line in my life evil cannot cross. And he always works out things for my good no matter how bad it gets. Nothing comes to me, no matter how hurtful or hard to take, that is beyond his ability to redeem and turn to good in my life. And he loves it when in the fight and the fury and the frustration, I say "yes". He loves it when the "Amen" (the "Okay, I surrender this to you") is said back to him by us to his glory.

So what happens when I say "yes" in times like that? According to Paul in this conversation with the Corinthians, the Lord anoints us, he sets his seal of ownership on us, he puts his Spirit in our hearts, and he gives us a guarantee that if we will keep saying "yes" to him, we will see more and greater things happening in our lives.

Do you want the kind of anointing Aaron had in the Old Testament, where they poured anointing oil on his head and all over him until it flowed off his beard and his robe and his fingers and his feet? Do you want the presence of God to be on you so much that everyone who comes in contact with you gets soaked by it? Learn to say "yes" to God.

Do you want to be marked by Christlikeness so much that everyone who knows you, knows that you belong to God? Do you know people like that? Do you want that in your life? Learn to say "yes" – tomorrow in the little things, learn to say "yes" to God.

Do you want to latch onto God's guarantee that he can make things happen in your life that are beyond your ability to even think or imagine? Learn to recognize his voice, hear what he has to say, and then say "yes" to him.

The life of surrender that leads into the deeper grace of sanctification is a life of learning to say "yes" to God.

CHAPTER TWENTY-THREE

HOLINESS EXPERIENCED

How We Can Lead Our People into the
Deeper Grace of the Sanctified Life

THE SANCTIFIED LIFE IS A LIFE THAT JUST
MAKES GOOD SENSE

Ephesians 4:17-5:2

When you think about it, and think about God, it only makes good sense that a concept like sanctification would be central to God's plan to have a close and abiding relationship with his people. He made a perfect human being who shared his character and enjoyed direct fellowship with him. That fellow fell and brought the whole thing crashing down on our heads. My friend Dan Loggins says, "When I get to heaven, the first thing I am going to do is walk up and sock Adam right in the kisser!" (Old Dan may have the shortest stay in paradise of anyone. I may get kicked out with him because I'll be right there, cheering him on.)

Something had to be done.

That something was the elaborate and costly plan of redemption, already in place, that does not stop short of the restoration of our fellowship with God, but includes the restoration of our character, and from that, the restoration of our relationships with each other. This is the work of God in us and he enables us to bring our part to it through our good sense response to him.

In a conversation with people like us who populated the church at Ephesus, Paul says, "Put on the new self, created to be like God in true righteousness and holiness." He is talking to Christians here, so it is safe to assume he is saying that there is more to be done in us than just transferring us from one kingdom to another, from one category to another.

Raymond S. Shelton was an old District Superintendent here in North Carolina when I was a young preacher boy. He became a real hero to me. He was raised on a farm in eastern Kentucky, outside the little town of Olive Hill. He was a short, fiery little guy, and as a young man was recruited by the horse racing industry to be a jockey, but God had other plans. He told this story on himself.

As a young boy, it was his job to mind the milk cow that the family owned. Basically, he was supposed to keep Old Bossy out of trouble while she grazed. That was not a very exciting assignment for a lively young man. The C&O Railway ran through their property on its way between Ashland and Lexington. For some reason, Bossy loved to roam the tracks. Well young Raymond had a solution for that. He tied a rope around that cow's neck and tied the other end to his ankle. That kept Bossy out of trouble and even allowed him to nap in the shade while she grazed in the sun.

Brilliant – except, Bossy kept pulling him out of the shade as she ventured after greener grass. The more that happened, the madder he got. Finally he had had enough. She pulled, he slid, and he got up and started running at her. She headed for the tracks. He came running up to her and kicked her as hard as he could, right in the side. She let out a bawl and away she went, running right down the tracks.

He said, "As I was bouncing down the tracks behind that crazy cow, I said to myself, 'Raymond, your temper has got you again. You definitely need more in your life than what you've got!'" Young Christian Raymond did need something more in his life. And he needed something less, as well. And he needed something else.

In his conversation with them, Paul is saying to the believers at the local church in Ephesus, and to us: You need a true righteousness, a true holiness in your life. You need something you cannot do for yourself. You need something you cannot work up in your own effort. You need something that only God and God alone can do for you and in you, so he can do what he wants to do in this world with you and through you.

That just makes good sense.

Paul tells us first what "holiness" is not.

He starts with them where the devil always starts with us. He reminds them of their past. Their old life, like ours, can be described by these eight characteristics.

In their past life, they were "darkened in their understanding", which is a fitting image of our culture and its lack of concern about who God is and how God desires for us to live.

In their past life, they were "separated from the life of God". In other words, before their new life in Christ they had been existing without really living to their full capacity.

In their past life, they were "ignorant", which is not a statement about their intelligence, but it means their minds might be filled with facts but they were choosing to ignore the truths that count forever.

In their past life, before their new life in Christ, they were "hardened in their hearts", which is the opposite of having a teachable spirit. The things of God just bounced off of them, like the seed in the parable bouncing off the beaten path.

In their past life, they were "insensitive to others" because of their self-centeredness.

In their past life, they were "given over to sensuality". That, my friends, is the world in which we live, captured in a phrase.

In their past life, they were "indulging in every kind of impurity". Nothing is sacred, nothing is prohibited, nothing is denied, nothing is out of bounds.

In their past life, before their new life in Christ, they were "continually lusting for more". They were living that dead and dried up life where there is no satisfaction, where we fall to the lie of enticement, where we are drawn in by the lure of temptation, where we are entrapped by the lust for just once more.

153

Everybody knows a true and faithful Christian is not characterized by this list of actions and attitudes. Occasionally we may stray into one of these areas, but we don't live there. That's Paul's point. In our past life, this is how we used to live. We do not live there anymore. That list of the characteristics of the old life is what "holiness" is not. It's something more. It's something less. It's something else. That just makes good sense.

Paul goes on to describe what else "holiness" is not.

In his conversation, he instructs us along with the saints in Ephesus, by the power of the Holy Spirit at work in us, to put off our old self and put on our new self. Walk away from the former way of life and walk in our new way of life.

Our new way of life is described by him as a series of 7 No's.

No Lying
Do you have a problem with handling the truth? Then you need to surrender that to God and allow him to help you with that. Confessing and apologizing immediately is usually painful enough, after you do it several times, to help you not want to have to keep doing it.

No Destructive Anger
Do you destroy your friendships and injure your family because of your anger? Then you need to ask God to temper your temper and turn that into passion for holy and healthy relationships.

No Foothold for the Devil
Do you play around with sin? Do you toy with temptation? Ask God to shine a light on those things so you can see just how ugly they really are, and where it is going to take you if you get caught up in it.

No Stealing
Do you have a problem being trustworthy with other people's property?

No Wicked Talk
Do you tell ethnic jokes? You need to stop. Do you gossip? You need to stop. Do you slice people to ribbons with your tongue? You need to

stop. Do you get in conversations with people inappropriately about matters that should be reserved for you and your spouse? You need to stop. Do you set the woods on fire by things you say? You need to stop.

No Activity that Grieves the Holy Spirit of God
How quick are you to obey?

No Violence
Violence here is described as bitterness, angry rage, brawling, slander, and every form of malice. You may say, "I really don't have a problem here." How much do you entertain yourself with it in the shows you watch, the movies you attend, the books you read? Ongoing exposure to violence scars and callouses a tender heart. Ask David.

That's a pretty strict set of expectations Paul is laying out there. But it's really not our list or even Paul's list. It's God's list through Paul. And, sorry, but it gets tougher than that. Paul would concede that the things he is saying we need to put off and put on would characterize a holy life. But he is very careful not to say, do these things and you will be holy.

It really is possible, by the sheer power of our will, to live this kind of life and not outwardly violate these prescriptions and prohibitions. But would you be holy? No. You would still be your old carnal self, polished up and shiny on the outside, but still full of death on the inside. We make a terrible mistake when we assume these actions and attitudes produce "holiness" in our lives. The scriptural truth is "holiness" in our lives will produce these actions and attitudes from the inside out, not from the outside in.

Too many people think, if I can just act better, I can become a better person, then God will be pleased with me, then I'll get to go to heaven when I die, all because I've been good. Really? Then what was the Cross all about? You can't save yourself. You can't clean yourself up. You can't make yourself acceptable to God. Only he can do that. And he does it through the shed blood of Christ on the cross, the power of his resurrection, and the presence of the Holy Spirit in your life.

One of my friends once said, 'We Wesleyans act like we're saved by grace but kept by keeping the law.'

It works from the inside out. God can do a work in our lives that will fundamentally change who we are which then changes how we act! That is the "new self" Paul is referring to, that is "created to be like God in true righteousness and holiness." It is something more. It is something less. It is something else. That just makes good sense.

So if it is not all these other attitudes and actions, then what is it?

"Holiness" is an ongoing operation of God's grace in an open and obedient heart that results in a lifestyle that honors God, a joy that is attractive and contagious, a character that reflects God's moral purity, a power inside that enables us to continue to become more and more like Christ and less and less like the person we used to be, an example that serves as proof to a watching world that there is truly something more, something less and something else available to them than the hopeless and helpless life they are living, and a compassion that compels and propels us outside these walls and into the broken places in our world.

What's the most broken place in your community? What are the most broken relationships in your community? Who are the most broken people in your community? If you as a person and as a church are not engaged there, you are not experiencing or practicing New Testament holiness.

As "imitators of God", we are going to be acting like God acts and doing what God would do, going where God would go and loving who God would love. As dearly loved children of God, we are compelled to share that love with others. Just as Christ loved us and gave himself up for us as a beautiful offering of sacrifice to God, so we will be pouring out our lives for others. If we are called to be like God, through the power of his Holy Spirit operating fully in our lives, it just makes good sense that we are going to love like he loves.

In a certain sidetracked era of our history, when we missed the point of the sanctified life and made it about us being holy for no other purpose than our personal holiness experience, we still enjoyed the blessings of God, still built strong churches and still saw people come to Christ. But we fell short of experiencing what we could have experienced had we stayed true to what holiness really is. It was something more than what we allowed ourselves to experience. It was something less than a bunch of the things we did experience, and impose on others. It was something else. It was God building a people to work with him to redeem the world in which he was so lovingly invested that he sent his one and only Son to save it, and bring eternal life to us all.

If all of this is true, it only makes good sense to learn from our mistakes and get ourselves back on a holiness path as a people and as a church.

John Sutherland Logan was pastor of the congregation that met at Speake Hall in London, a church once pastored by the legendary Oswald Chambers. He was the first non-Anglican to be named a chaplain to the Queen. He was among a group of British pastors being addressed by the Chinese apostle, Watchman Nee. Someone had asked Pastor Nee to define "holiness". Logan said he went around the room, placing his hands on each pastor's head in succession, saying, "Holiness is the Spirit of Christ in me, plus the Spirit of Christ in you, plus the Spirit of Christ in you, plus the Spirit of Christ in you . . . ." Logan said everyone got the point, they thought. Then he began back around the room, saying, "Less the self in me, less the self in you, less the self in you, less the self in you . . . ."

"Holiness" is an ongoing surrender to God's character-forming work in you, that allows more and more of the dynamic development of the person he is making you to be, while helping you be less of the person you used to be, plus releasing you to the work God is calling you to do in partnership with him.

Do you need something more in your life beyond what you now have? Do you need something less in your life because the things you are allowing to fill your life are taking you further from Christ rather than closer to Christ? Do you need something else in your life because what you are experiencing now is not measuring up to what you need?

Are you hungry for a deeper walk, a deeper life, a greater impact? You can have it. God is calling you to it. It only makes good sense to pursue it.

CHAPTER TWENTY-FOUR

HOLINESS EXPERIENCED

How We Can Lead Our People into the
Deeper Grace of the Sanctified Life

THE SANCTIFIED LIFE IS A LIFE OF INNER PEACE

The Strong Man
Luke 11:21-22

Jesus said, "When a strong man, fully armed, guards his own house, his possessions are safe. But when someone stronger attacks and overpowers him, he takes away the armor in which the man trusted and divides up the spoils.'

I live in Kernersville, North Carolina, known as the heart of the Golden Triad. We are a booming bedroom community for the cities of Winston-Salem to our west, Greensboro to our east, and High Point to our south. We are home to FedEx's southeastern hub, and our international airport, ten minutes away, boasts the longest runway between Washington D.C. and Miami.

Back in the day, for us Wesleyans, Kernersville was the heart of the Pilgrim Holiness Church in the south. The strongest district in the southern area of the Pilgrim Holiness Church developed in North Carolina. The district spread into Virginia and South Carolina, and eventually those districts were established out of what had been renamed the Southern District. But what really made Kernersville the heart of the church in the south was the establishing of Southern Pilgrim College.

Southern Pilgrim was a four-year Bible college with a two-year junior college and a four-year high school. Along with many from North

Carolina, people came from Maryland, Virginia, West Virginia, Kentucky, Tennessee, South Carolina and Florida for ministerial training at the school. I came all the way from Ohio, where my dad was pastoring at the time. A great many found a home in North Carolina and stayed, strengthening the North Carolina District even more.

At the time, Kernersville was a sleepy little town whose only claim to fame was a Ray's Kingburger and Snow's Diner. We had Spiro's Pizza downtown, too, but we weren't allowed to go there because Bill sold beer (but that pizza was great!). R.J. Reynolds had a bunch of tobacco warehouses on the east side of town, across the street from the school, and when I-40 came through, skirting the south side of the campus, Roadway and Pilot trucking companies built large terminals here.

Today, Kernersville has been discovered and is growing beyond what anyone would have imagined back then. The downtown is alive. David Fitzpatrick has resurrected Snow's iconic tiny diner (now Fitz' on Main). There are consignments shops, boutiques, antique stores, restaurants and law offices downtown. Cakes and All Things Yummy provides the aromatic atmosphere. We even have a Doggie Bakery for dog treats in one block and a Cat Café (yes, really) in the next block. If those clients ever cross paths, it will be a catastrophe.

One of the down sides to this growth is that there seems to be an unwritten rule, apparently, that everyone within twenty miles of Kernersville must drive through downtown between the hours of 3:00 pm and 7:00 pm every Friday. Pity the fool who is in a hurry and gets caught in that line of traffic.

The traffic meets at the heart of Kernersville, the intersection of Main Street going north and south, and Mountain Street going east and west. This has been the heart of the community for a long time. There is a large boulder on the sidewalk on the northeast corner with an ancient, heavy brass tablet bolted to it. It reads, "Site of Dobson's Tavern. Here George Washington breakfasted June 2, 1791."

Hanging in the center of that intersection is a traffic light. It has red, yellow and green lensed lights on each of four sides. Astonishingly unimposing, that light wields awesome power. When your light is green you go. When it is red you stop. When it is yellow, depending on your personality, the content of your character, or the urgency of your mission, you either slow down or speed up. Everyone plays by those rules. The light has no such power in itself. But it has authority. That authority is duly established and any who would doubt that can write their checks for the ticket to the fine city of Kernersville.

In addition, (we'll assume him male) should a certain person, dressed in dark blue pants and a white shirt, wearing a gold badge on his chest, step into the middle of that intersection and raise his hand, all traffic would come to an immediate halt. And he can stand there until he backs up traffic in Colfax or Horneytown if he wants to. Everyone stops. Not because he has more strength than the car or truck you are riding in, because he doesn't. You stop because he has the authority to stop you. You know he has the authority, and if you are good-hearted, you assume he has a good reason. He is doing what he is doing for the good of Kernersville.

I was sitting in that traffic one day in the left turn lane going south, waiting for the light to change so I could turn east onto Mountain Street. A Fat Boy Harley came into the intersection going west, swerved a little to his right, and came to a dead stop in front of me and the car in the southbound lane beside me. The rider was wearing a sleeveless black leather vest with stitched-on writing on the back, blue jeans, black engineer boots, and a military style World War II German Army helmet. He had a bushy grey mustache and chin beard and was wearing dark wrap-around sunglasses. His lady was perched on the seat behind him wearing her biker best.

Immediately, a long line of motorcycles, mostly Harleys and Indians with a couple of Hondas thrown in, began to come roaring through the intersection. There must have been thirty or forty of them in a long line. The light turned green but no one moved, except the line of bikes. The light cycled through again, and they still came. No one moved but them. Finally, the last one rolled by, the throaty sound from the exhaust echoing from the walls of the buildings, and our Strong Man roared away at the tail of the line – without even a wave or a nod.

And the heart of Kernersville returned to normal.

The Strong Man on the motorcycle had no authority to do what he did, to impose his personal will onto the heart of Kernersville, but he took the authority to do it. And he held the heart of Kernersville captive to his will. Had our friend with the badge come along, you know he would have taken authority from the one who had usurped it, even though he probably would have allowed the parade of bikes to pass on through. But there would have been no question about who the Stronger Man was. And if the Strong Man had resisted or disrespected the Stronger Man, the Strong Man, fully armed in his Harley gear and sitting astride his Harley bike, would have found those things in which he trusted being taken away from him by the Stronger Man who would have possessed his possessions – his cash and bike – with full authority (both the right and the power) to do so.

In your life before Christ, the Strong Man possessed you and made his home in the heart of your life. The Stronger Man arrived and evicted him, taking you into his possession and blessing you to an even greater measure than the Strong Man had abused you. You were set free.

But eventually you discovered that the Strong Man does not give up easily, and he came crawling back around, crouching at your door, waiting for any opportunity to disrupt your life, sow seeds of discord and distrust, try to bring disaster down upon you, and repossess you if he could. And, you sadly discovered, he had a treacherous ally living in the heart of your life. Call it whatever you will, there remained a part of you that was governed by your self-will and responded all too readily to your selfish ambition, self-pride, self-importance, need for self-promotion and self-preservation, and was firmly rooted in your self-centered orientation. Pogo was right. "We have met the enemy and he is us!"

Just to clarify: We ourselves are not the Enemy with a capital "E", but we are often our own worst enemy as we allow way too much interference to take place from the capital "E" Enemy, the Strong Man the Stronger Man ousted.

We need the Stronger Man to take such a position in the heart of our lives that his authority reigns within us – both the right and the power to defeat the Strong Man. And that authority is ceded by us to him as we live in relationship with him day-by-day, hour-by-hour, moment-by-moment, decision-by-decision. And when we relapse into the "flesh" – pulled back into that self-centeredness – he has plenty of access and plenty of persuasive skill to pull us back into line. And he will.

So the issue is, to whom will we cede authority in the heart of our life?

In his deep and rich book of daily spiritual nourishment, *This Day with The Master*, Methodist scholar and holiness preacher Dennis Kinlaw makes this astute observation about the cleverness of the enemy in deceiving us to get us to cede the authority in the heart of our life over to him:

> Satan disguises submission to himself under the ruse of personal autonomy. He never asks us to become his servants. Never once did the serpent say to Eve, "I want to be your master." The shift in commitment is never from Christ to evil; it is always from Christ to self. And instead of his will, self-interest now rules and what I want reigns. And that is the essence of sin.

Jesus said, "All authority in heaven and on earth has been given to me." That supersedes any usurped authority of any Strong Man who tries to make claim to any area of your life. And it applies to your own God-given sovereignty over your life. By virtue of creation and the cross, resurrection and redemption, sacrifice and surrender, it belongs to him. And you alone have the power to give it back to him.

How smoothly your life runs, how much of a lasting good comes from your life, how well you bless the other people in your life, and how close you come to fulfilling the purpose for which you were created depends directly on how well you cede authority to the One who is the Stronger Man residing in the heart of your life. That will be the key to inner peace for you.

CHAPTER TWENTY-FIVE

HOLINESS EXPERIENCED

How We Can Lead Our People into the Deeper Grace of the Sanctified Life

THE LIFE OF SANCTIFICATION IS A LIFE OF SACRIFICE

Matthew 23:23-24
Romans 12:1-2

How can we help our people embrace the grace of a sacrificial spirit that is so like God?

In Matthew 23:23-24, Jesus says to the religious leaders of his day, and us, "Woe to you, teachers of the Law and Pharisees, you hypocrites! You give a tenth of your spices – mint, dill and cummin. But you have neglected the more important matters of the Law – justice, mercy and faithfulness. You should have practiced the latter, without neglecting the former. You blind guides! You strain out a gnat but swallow a camel."

In Romans 12:1-2, Paul says to the Christians of his day, and us, "Therefore I urge you, brothers [and sisters], in view of God's mercy, to offer your bodies as living sacrifices, holy and pleasing to God – which is your spiritual worship. Do not conform any longer to the pattern of this world, but be transformed by the renewing of your mind. Then you will be able to test and approve what God's will is – his good, pleasing and perfect will."

At first glance, there may not seem to be any direct correlation between these two statements, but deeper reflection will show that Jesus and Paul are actually addressing the same issue – sacrifice that is acceptable to God.

These passages are two sides of the same coin. Jesus is saying, "Here's how not to do it." Paul is saying, "Here is how to do it."

Jesus is referring to the statement by the Old Testament prophet Micah, who wrote, "What does the Lord require of you? To act justly, and to love mercy and to walk humbly with your God." When we look at this in the context of Jesus' strong rebuke to these religious people for how they totally missed the spirit of their Heavenly Father in how they handled the gifts he poured into their lives, it should cause us to do a little heart check ourselves on that, as well. If there were Jewish "holiness" people, this would be them.

It is as one pastor said, that Jesus both tells it like it is, but also shows us how it should be. He calls out the sin, but also carves out the way.

God wants to develop his character in us, which will find its way out in our lives through a spirit of sacrifice. Sacrifice is a central, essential component of our sanctifying relationship with God – his sacrifice for us, and our sacrifice for him. There is no relationship with God without sacrifice. It is so central to our relationship that the scriptures describe Jesus as "the Lamb slain from the foundation of the world." Every lamb that was sacrificed in the old sacrificial system was not only pointing forward to the sacrifice of Christ on the cross, but back to the eternal sacrifice of the precious Lamb of God, from before time began. The writer to the Hebrews declares this sacrifice was "once for all" – for all people, for all time, for all sin. Hebrews 10:10 declares that "we have been made holy through the sacrifice of the body of Jesus Christ once for all."

Building on this concept of his sacrifice for us leading us to embrace the joy of sacrifice for him, Paul tells the Philippian church, "Do nothing out of selfish ambition or vain conceit, but in humility consider others better than yourselves. Each of you should look not only to your own interests, but also to the interests of others. In your relationships with one another, have the same mindset as Christ Jesus: who, being in very nature God, did not consider equality with God something to be used to his own advantage; rather he made himself nothing by taking the very nature of a servant, being made in human likeness, and being found in appearance as a man, he humbled himself by becoming obedient to death – even death on a cross!"

We have no relationship with God without sacrifice – his once for all in Christ, and ours daily, even moment by moment, as we live in obedience to him, with his word in our minds and his Spirit in our hearts.

And this spirit of sacrifice is to characterize not only our relationship with him, but also our relationships with each other. Because I love and serve Christ, who gave himself for me, that ought to impact how I treat you. Abraham Lincoln said it this way, "I care not for a man's religion whose dog and cat are not the better for it." If I treat my pets better because I love the Lord, I'll treat you better, too. And I'll do it, no matter how you treat me. By the help of God's Holy Spirit abiding fully in me, I will return unkindness with kindness, misrepresentation with grace, misunderstanding with understanding, and hatred with love. And when you need something, and I have it, I'll give it to you, whether you can ever pay me back or not. That is just the Spirit of Christ living in us and living out of us. It is a generous unselfish spirit that embraces the joy of sacrifice.

In the context of a sacrificial spirit that puts others before ourselves, as Christ did for us, can you understand why Jesus would be so frustrated with religious pretenders who would reduce a relationship with God to such an earthbound formula as to say, "Look how holy I am. I even give a tenth of my salt and pepper in the offering at church!"?

Hypocrites are people who act one way on the outside, but their internal motivation is twisted and hidden from view and turned back in on their own selfish interests. That's how it was with these religious professionals. Hypocrites are people who say God acts one way, usually reducible to a formula that favors them, and imply that you just don't measure up, when all the time God is standing right in front of them saying, "You're missing the whole point!"

Hypocrites are people who find ways to make painless sacrifices.

When you are the Lamb of God slain from the foundation of the world, and you are on your way to be dragged out of town and nailed to a piece of wood and left hanging there until you die, and you meet these people who refuse to shed a tear for hurting people – and never a drop of blood – you probably would not be very charitable toward them, would you? Especially if you knew they would be the ones driving the "crucify him" agenda. For this reason, Jesus emphasizes the grace of a sacrificial spirit in contrast to selfish religion, and drags their sin right out into the open, points at it and calls it what it is, and calls them to a higher and deeper relationship with God.

"Let us fix our eyes on Jesus, the author and perfecter of our faith, who for the joy set before him endured the cross, scorning its shame, and sat down at the right hand of the throne of God." (Hebrews 12:2)

Jesus draws us away from self-centered religion to the joy we find in following him. It is an upward spiraling pattern of growth. When we embrace the joy of sanctified selfless sacrifice, we experience the grace of a generous spirit. As we experience the grace of a generous spirit, we are drawn to the joy we find in sanctified selfless sacrifice. When we let go, open our hands, release who we are and what we have to God and those around us, we experience the blessings of God in a way we never imagined.

This is what I told a young Carolina student years ago, who was struggling with his faith, not sure he could really trust God with his life and future: "There is no guarantee to this, but much more often than not, when we give to God the things we love the most, he has a beautiful way of turning around and giving them back to us in a way we never dreamed was possible. It's not your things he wants. It's you."

God has wired us to be like him, and when we consistently practice in our lifestyles the characteristics of our generous God, we flourish. When we do not, we turn inward, shrivel, and die. These are the more important matters of justice and mercy and faithfulness Jesus spoke of to the Pharisees and desires of us. Through his mercy God acts to bring about our justification, our salvation, through his Son. In that same spirit, we offer ourselves in sacrifice for others until there is justice in their world, mercy in their life, faithfulness in their heart.

According to Paul in Romans 12:1-2, that is the essence of our true and proper worship. The living sacrifice we offer is truly an acceptable way to worship God. It is marked by an orientation toward God, and an orientation toward others. This is what the teachers of the Law and the Pharisees completely missed in Jesus' day.

For them, worship was the religious exercise of rituals acted out in hope of making themselves acceptable to God. Even to the point, in their minds, of impressing God with the attention to detail that characterized their religious activity. Unfortunately, burrowing so far down into such less important aspects of religion and missing out completely on the more important aspects of righteous relationships makes a religious person proud because these trivialities can actually be accomplished without God's help and at little personal cost. It makes a religious person pompous because the rest of us can be shown how we are being out-performed in religious fervor. And it makes a religious person a pain because it's meaningless to the real work of God in the world and it gets in the way in all kinds of ways.

Paul, in Romans 12:1, describes the kind of worship God desires from us, and you don't find anything about tithed spices anywhere near this passage. He says, "Therefore, I urge you brothers and sisters, in view of God's mercy, to offer yourselves as living sacrifices, holy and pleasing to God – which is your spiritual worship" (or as the Old Version says, "your reasonable service").

"Reasonable service." I take that to mean, in view of God's mercy offered to us in the sacrifice of Christ for us, living like this, as an offering poured out in worship daily for him, is the only way to live that makes sense. In view of God's mercy. It has nothing to do with religion. It has everything to do with our relationship with God and the people he has brought into our lives. When we trust him fully with our life, we learn the grace of a sacrificial spirit, which opens us to the wonderful discovery of the joy of serving him – a sacrificial service that brings a sense of honor to our lives, a sense of purpose to our lives, a sense of being part of something way bigger than us to our lives. Who wouldn't want that?

And how does it work itself out in my personal behavior and my horizontal relationships? New Testament scholar J.B. Philips states Paul's application of this truth this way, in his paraphrase of Romans 12:9-10. "Let us have no imitation Christian love. Let us have a genuine break with evil and a real devotion to good. Let us have real warm affection for one another as between brothers [and sisters], and a willingness to let the other [person] have the credit."

Do you get it? The big picture is, when God gets us he gets all we hold in our hands. It's not about him having to pry it out of our hands in order to bless someone else with it. It's not about me deciding to give him things that do not really matter or cost me next to nothing to give, while I hold onto the really good stuff. It's about me living in such a relationship with him that I know if he needs it and I have it, he can have it. If it turns out I need it, he will give it back to me abundantly. I just need to trust him and obey him.

The more important matters of justice and mercy and faithfulness are what the religious people missed. Justice tempered with mercy flows out of the faithfulness of God to his promises and as such to us. Jesus was talking to them about these deep truths, and then went and demonstrated it in his sacrificial act of love. And it is a characteristic mark of all those who are fully devoted to him, and sanctified by his Spirit.

In contrast, fear is not a mark of those who are fully devoted to him, and sanctified by his Spirit. Fear is demotivating and it is a great tool of the enemy to keep us from experiencing deeper and greater blessings in our relationship with God. That is why he has given us faith. Faith is a gift from God. It is not something we muster up from within. It comes from God. And faith is the antidote to fear.

Fear knocked at the door. Faith answered. There was no one there.

Our whole relationship with God is a faith venture. But it is not about how much faith we have. Ever see a mustard seed? It is about in whom our faith is placed. We can surrender to the will of God without fear. His will is good, pleasing and perfect. In fact, if we could see eternal realities beyond our limited view of life, we would actually be afraid not to trust God.

These are the more important matters for us, the call to walk faithfully (humility) with God in integrity (justice) and love (mercy). This is what the Pharisees and teachers of the Law missed. There is a life of unmatched

168

fellowship to be found in the cultivation of a faithful, loving, authentic spirit. That's a lot better than empty religion could ever do for us. Besides, if being religious is like swallowing a camel, and if a camel tastes as bad as a camel smells, who wants that? No wonder some of those rules-bound old-timers had such a sour look on their faces.

C.T. Studd was not one of them.

C.T. Studd was from a rich, prominent family in Great Britain. He was a world-famous cricket player of another generation. (Cricket is what baseball would look like if politicians had invented it. It makes no sense but it gets everybody excited.) He became a Christian through the influence of his father who was converted in a D.L. Moody evangelistic service. His faith was so strong that he denounced his sizable inheritance and launched out into a sacrificial life of foreign missionary work, first with Hudson Taylor in China, then in India, and later in internal Africa. You should read his story. You may have read a couple of his famous sayings.

Have you heard, "Only one life, will soon be past. Only what's done for Christ will last"? That's C.T. Studd. How about, "Some want to live within the sound of church or chapel bell. I want to run a rescue shop within a yard of hell"? That's C.T. Studd.

He gave his whole life as a sacrifice for Christ, prayed in his support across all those years, and died on the field in what was then the Congo at the age of 70.

My all-time favorite quote from C.T. Studd is this: "If Jesus Christ be God and died for me, then no sacrifice can be too great for me to make for him." C.T. Studd got it. When God works his miracle of sanctifying grace in us and sanctifies our whole heart and life, he develops in us a heart like his, marked by integrity flowing from his justice, love flowing from his mercy, and humble fellowship with him flowing from his faithfulness.

> I have one deep, supreme desire, that I may be like Jesus.
> To this I fervently aspire, that I may be like Jesus.
> I want my heart his throne to be so that a watchful world may see
> His likeness shining forth in me. I want to be like Jesus.

He spent his life in doing good. I want to be like Jesus.
Always in humble service stood. I want to be like Jesus.
He sympathized with hearts distressed.
He spoke the words that cheered and blessed.
He welcomed sinners to his breast. I want to be like Jesus.

A holy, blameless life he led. I want to be like Jesus.
The Father's will, his drink and bread. I want to be like Jesus.
And when at last he came to die, "Father, forgive them" he could cry,
For those who taunt and crucify. I want to be like Jesus.

O perfect life of Christ my Lord. I want to be like Jesus.
My recompense and my reward, that I may be like Jesus.
His Spirit fill my hung'ring soul, his power all my life control,
My deepest prayer, my highest goal, that I may be like Jesus.

– Thomas Obediah Chisholm (1866-1960)

CHAPTER TWENTY-SIX

HOLINESS EXPERIENCED

How We Can Lead Our People into the Deeper Grace of the Sanctified Life

THE LIFE OF SANCTIFICATION IS LIFE
AS IT WAS MEANT TO BE LIVED

This Is the Will of God for You
1 Thessalonians 4:3a
1 Thessalonians 5:23-24

In his first written conversation with the Christians in the Greek city of Thessalonica, people like us, the Apostle Paul makes a couple of very bold, declarative statements about sanctification.

The first is, "It is God's will that you should be holy."

The second is in the form of a prayer. "May God himself, the God of peace, sanctify you through and through. May your whole spirit, soul and body be kept blameless at the coming of our Lord Jesus Christ. The one who calls you is faithful and he will do it."

The term "holy" has been around a long time. It shows up as a word being used in the context of the religions of the Ancient Near East. It originally meant "to be set apart for special use." We would expect the utensils in Israel's Temple to be "holy" (set apart to be used only in the worship of Yahweh), but so were the utensils in the Temples of Baal among the Phoenicians, or the Temple of Dagon among David's harassers the Philistines, or the Temple of Marduk in Babylon, or the Temple of Ra in Egypt. Where the Canaanite goddess Asherah was worshipped, the cult prostitutes were designated as "holy".

If I remember correctly, there was no moral dimension given to this term until it began to be applied to the God of Israel and the things that were consecrated to the God of Israel.

By the time of Paul, the dual understanding of the term, both set apart and morally pure, was well established. This is what Paul is referring to when he says to be holy is God's will, God's design, God's desire for us. Our character being like his character, our lives being set apart for special use and morally pure. Since God is deeply invested in everything that is in our best interest, us being holy is important to him. His investment in us, of course, comes in the person of his Son, Jesus Christ. That's a pretty big investment.

According to Paul, in Romans 8:29, God's plan from the beginning for his children was that they be like Christ. But holiness is a puzzle to us. It is not our natural inclination, which because of the fall is towards evil. "Prone to wander, Lord I feel it. Prone to leave the God I love." That's our nature prior to our conversion. Unfortunately, it's also our nature after our conversion, since we still tend to battle with being prideful, self-centered and driven by selfish ambition and self-interest. Something needs to happen inside us to break that downward pull away from God.

Paul's prayer for us is to be sanctified through and through. Paul believes God himself, the God of peace, is on a personal mission to bring this about in our lives. In war, peace comes when someone surrenders. Someone lays down his or her arms. Someone gives up their claim to sovereignty and allows himself or herself to be placed under the sovereignty of the victor. To be at war with Almighty God is not a good thing. Who believes they are going to win that one? But in this case, the Almighty God is also the faithful God. He is faithful to his character, which is holy love. He is faithful to his mission, which is to bring us into a loving and enriching relationship with him, no longer enslaved by sin, but restored in relationship with him to be his children. He is faithful to his integrity, tempering justice with mercy and forgiving us of all our sin. And he is faithful to everyone else who is lost and away from him, using us in our redeemed and restored relationship to build bridges into their lives, assured that when we do, Jesus will walk across them.

What this work of sanctification does is break our orientation to ourselves as the center of our universe, and reorient us to our proper relationship with God, which is how we were created to live. Paul did not know Copernicus, but Paul is calling for us to have a Copernican revolution. Nicolaus Copernicus was a Renaissance era mathematician and astronomer who figured out that the sun did not revolve around the earth, but that the earth actually revolved around the sun. That couldn't be right. Everyone saw it every day. The sun came up in the east, traveled across the sky, and set in the west. Every day. But by mathematical genius, he figured out that the sun actually travels on a trajectory through space and carries the earth in orbit with it. The religious leaders, of course, immediately branded him a heretic and nearly burned him at the stake. But others came forward, confirmed his theory to be true, and the lucky fellow escaped a gruesome death.

This revolutionized the science of his day. This changed everything.

In our natural process of maturing, we move from an early understanding that the whole world revolves around us to eventually becoming aware that there actually are other people in the world, and they are not there to serve us. Bummer. Most of us make this journey in maturity without a whole lot of trouble. Some of us never do quite make it. In our spiritual journey, as we grow in grace through the sanctifying power of the Holy Spirit working in us, we are less prone to exalt ourselves and more prone to exalt the Lord. We are less prone to look out for our own interests at the expense of others, and more prone to put others first. If, as Dietrich Bonhoeffer declared, Jesus is "The Man for Others", shouldn't we become men and women who are known to sacrifice ourselves for others?

This call to holy living is what God desires for us and offers to us. It is the way we were meant to live. But there is one critical element Paul is certain to point out to us. "The one who calls you is faithful, and he will do it." It is important to understand that it is God who is calling us, and it is God who will make it happen, not us. It is also important to understand what God is calling us to, and what he desires to do.

He is not calling us to perfect performance. He is calling us to have a relationship with him.

Regardless of our capacities or limitations, we can all have a relationship with God. In our relationship with him, we follow him. We live in fellowship with him. We develop our companionship with him. And this is how we get to know him. And this is how we get to the places he wants us to go in our spiritual life. And we soon learn, if we are going to have a relationship with him, he sets the pace, he sets the direction, he calls the starts and the stops. This relationship, this walk, is with him. "Can two walk together except they be agreed?" the Old Testament prophet asked.

Spiritually speaking, our relationship with God, our growth in righteousness, is done through a process of what the New Testament calls "sanctification" or "growth in grace and knowledge". As we put off certain habits, thought patterns, actions and words we discover are not like him, and we learn to put on other habits, thought patterns, actions and words we discover are like him, we grow in our relationship with him. These can be attitudes, abilities, actions, activities, or ambitions that are either pleasing or not pleasing to the Lord. He will say, "Watch your step here," or "Come a little closer here," or "Don't do that," or "Don't step in that!"

We are called to discard characteristics of our old life that are contrary to the character of Christ – things like grudges, hatred, dishonesty, unfaithfulness, bad language, a spirit of materialism, immorality, stubbornness, laziness, impure thoughts, or that other thing you know you should not be doing but are. That thing you thought of just now. We are called to add characteristics to our new life that are consistent with the character of Christ – things like generosity, restitution, wholesome relationships in our family, helping others, submission, devotion, sharing our faith, consistency, integrity, mercy or that other thing you know you should be doing but aren't. That thing you thought of just now. As you mature, you will discover that you will tend to have less trouble with temptations related to sins of the flesh (except maybe overeating), and more struggle with sins of the spirit – those intangible but real things like anger, jealousy, pride, selfishness, or a temptation to shade the truth in your favor.

And that is how we grow in our relationship with him. He will guide us in putting off things that are unnecessary or harmful or wrong, things that are contrary to the character of Christ, and he will lead us in putting on things that are helpful and healthy and holy, things that are consistent with the character of Christ. You will not be far into this relationship before you realize your list of expectations is different than your friends' lists. We grow at different paces. We have different affinities and addictions. We are not all at the same place at the same time. Focus on your list and let them and the Lord take care of their list.

I mentioned addictions. We are all addiction inclined. We are wired to be people of habit. That was originally intended to be for our good. The fall twisted that, and now it usually works in a powerful way against us. Let me say two things about that: the depth of forgiveness and transformation in Christ goes deeper than the grip of addiction on our lives, and the power of his resurrection is greater than the power of addiction in our life. God will break and then sanctify the power of addiction in your life and help you develop holy habits. As you grow in grace and knowledge, God will lead you faithfully into deeper grace and more knowledge. As God leads you faithfully into deeper grace and more knowledge, you will continue to grow faithfully into deeper grace and more knowledge.

Will you ever mess up? Will you never trip and fall? I suppose in your physical life right now, as an accomplished walker of a good number of years, it could be possible that you could walk the rest of your life and never trip and fall. Really. You have the skills. You have the experience. You have the confidence. But you also have the past performance that predicts the unlikely chance of such a future result as never falling again as long as you live. You're not likely to be a perfect performance walker. Like the rest of us, you're going to fall. I'm talking about the physical act of walking here. Have you tripped and fallen lately?

> "There is nothing that can quite compare
> With treading on a step that isn't there."

Possibility and probability are two different things. Yes, it is possible that you might never trip and fall ever again in your life. But it's not really likely. Our poor past performance and our tendency toward clumsiness, plus the law of gravity, goes against us here, doesn't it?

Paul talks about us being "blameless" in our relationship with God and those around us. That is an important concept for us to grasp. It has to do with our intentions, the purity of our motives, and not so much about the unbroken perfection of our performance. I can mean to do well and still mess up. If that happens and my transgression is against God, I need to repent, get back up and continue living in fellowship with him. He made me. He knows I am dust. I can mean to do well and still mess up in my relationships with friends, family or complete strangers. I didn't mean for it to turn out the way it did. If that happens, I need to apologize immediately, seek forgiveness, and then continue living in fellowship with that person. It's not about perfect performance. It's about a pure heart. Not faultless, but blameless.

And his grace reaches every corner of our lives – body, soul and spirit.

God is speaking to us boldly through Paul. He is assuring us it is possible to live life like we were designed to live it, in a meaningful, joyful, rewarding relationship with him that helps us become more and more like Christ and less and less like the person we used to be. And that is a place from which we can make a major contribution to the cause of the kingdom, and in the lives of the people all around us.

There is a paraphrase of Isaiah 45:19 that reads, "And I didn't tell Israel to ask me for what I didn't plan to give." If God himself inspired Paul to pray that prayer that God himself, the God of peace, would sanctify us through and through, do you think he doesn't intend to do it? You sincerely pray that prayer consistently, every day, and you will find your life being transformed in ways you could hardly imagine from where you are sitting at this moment.

This is the will of God for you. He is faithful. He will do it.

CONCLUSION

Jasmin was sitting in on the final ordination interview for her husband, Lyle, which was our custom. As we were talking with Lyle about his understanding and experience of sanctification, Jasmin spoke up. Her confession was, "I really don't understand sanctification. All I know is, I spent a whole lot of my life riding the fence. Which side of the fence I was on depended on who I was with. I got really tired of that and one day I decided to get down off the fence and take off running in God's direction, as fast and as far as I could go. That has made all the difference in my life." After a moment of silence, I spoke up and said, "Jasmin, I think you may just understand sanctification better than some of our pastors do."

This is God's will for you. He said it plainly in his Word. And his Word is saturated with this truth. He draws you to himself, and as you draw near to him you discover that a sincere and dedicated act of consecration on your part will be met with his sanctifying grace. He will fill every space in your life you make available to him. As badly as you want this, he wants it even more for you. The life we are talking about is a matter of the heart. See if this doesn't speak to the heart of the matter for you.

Rabindranath Tagore was a Nobel Prize winning author, poet and philosopher of Bengali descent from India. He did not claim to be a Christian, but somehow I believe he might just have known Christ on some level. Listen to what he said in *Song Offerings*.

> I had gone a-begging from door to door in the village path, when thy golden chariot appeared in the distance like a gorgeous dream, and I wondered who was this King of all kings?
>
> My hope rose high and I thought my evil days were at an end, and I stood waiting for the alms to be given unasked and for wealth scattered on all sides in the dust.
>
> Thy chariot stopped where I stood. Thy glance fell on me and thou camedst down with a smile. I felt that the luck of my life had come

at last. Then of a sudden thou didst hold out thy right hand and say, "What hast thou to give to me?"

Ah, what a kingly jest it was to open thy palm to a beggar to beg! I was confused and stood undecided, and then from my wallet I slowly took out the least little grain of corn and gave it to thee.

But how great my surprise when at the day's end I emptied my bag on the floor to find a least little gram of gold among the poor heap. I bitterly wept, and wished that I had had the heart to give thee my all.

Do I dare give myself to God the way he has given himself to me? What would happen if I did?

This life. This life of being sanctified through and through. It is for real. It is for now. It is for you.

Grace to all who love our Lord Jesus Christ with an undying love.
Ephesians 6:24

BIBLIOGRAPHY

Bainton, Roland H., *Here I Stand: A Life of Martin Luther*, Penguin Publishing Group, London, 1955

Black, Robert, *How Firm a Foundation*, Wesleyan Publishing House, Indianapolis, IN, 2006

Black, Robert, and Wayne A. Caldwell, "A Church Called Freedom's Hill" pamphlet, Southern Wesleyan University publisher, Central, SC, 2003

Black, Robert and Keith W. Drury, *The Story of The Wesleyan Church*, Wesleyan Publishing House, Indianapolis, IN, 2012

Casey, Anthony, "The Hermeneutics of Moral Reasoning: Theological and Moral Reasoning in the Context of Conflicting Histories of Race Relations in The Wesleyan Church", unpublished doctoral research paper, Trinity International University, Deerfield, IL, 2016

Cook, Thomas, *New Testament Holiness*, Epworth Press, London, (1906) 1963

Crooks, Adam, *The American Wesleyan*, weekly religious periodical, Wesleyan Methodist Publishing House, Syracuse, New York, February 6, 1867

Dayton, Donald W., *Discovering an Evangelical Heritage*, Baker Academic Books, Peabody, MA, 1976

Dayton, Donald W., *Theological Roots of Pentecostalism*, Francis Asbury Press of Zondervan Publishing House, Grand Rapids, 1987

DeNeff, Steve and David Drury, *Soul Shift: The Measure of a Life Transformed*, Wesleyan Publishing House, Indianapolis, IN, 2011

Drury, Keith W., *Holiness for Ordinary People*, Wesleyan Publishing House, Indianapolis, IN, 1983

Drury, Keith W., "The Holiness Movement is Dead", unpublished paper presented to the Christian Holiness Association convention, 1995

Drury, Keith W. and David Drury, *Ageless Faith: A Conversation between Generations about Church*, Wesleyan Publishing House, Indianapolis, IN, 2010

Emerson, Michael O. and Christian Smith, *Divided by Faith: Evangelical Religion and the Problem of Race in America*, Oxford University Press, New York, NY, 2000

Haines, Lee W., *Reformers and Revivalists: Wesleyan History Series*, Wesleyan Publishing House, Indianapolis, IN, 1993

Henry, Carl F. H., *The Uneasy Conscience of Modern Fundamentalism*, William B. Eerdmans Publishing Company, Grand Rapids, MI, (1947) 2003

Kenneth Cain Kinghorn, *The Story of Asbury Theological Seminary*, Emeth Press, Lexington, KY, 2010

Kinlaw, Dennis with Christiane A. Albertson, *This Day With The Master*, Francis Asbury Press of Zondervan Publishing House, Grand Rapids, 2002

Knapp, Martin Wells, *Lightning Bolts from Pentecostal Skies; or Devices of the Devil Unmasked*, Revivalist Press, Cincinnati, OH, 1898

LeRoy, Matthew W. and Jeremy Summers, *Awakening Grace: Spiritual Practices to Transform Your Soul*, Wesleyan Publishing House, Indianapolis, IN, 2012

Nicholson, Roy S., *Wesleyan Methodism in the South: Being a Story of Eighty-Six Years of Reform and Religious Activities in the South as Conducted by the American Wesleyans*, Wesleyan Methodist Publishing House, Syracuse, NY, 1933

Rees, Paul S., *Seth Cook Rees: Warrior Saint*, Pilgrim Holiness Publishing House, Indianapolis, IN, 1934

Russell Times, local newspaper (now defunct), Times Publishing Company, Russell, KY

Schwartz, Kristin, *3 Colors of Ministry: A Trinitarian Approach to Identifying and Developing Your Spiritual Gifts*, ChurchSmart Resources, Bloomington, MN, 2001

Shuster, Philip, Eugene L. Huddleston and Alvin Staufer, *C&O Power: Steam and Diesel Locomotives of the Chesapeake and Ohio Railway 1900-1965*, Alvin Staufer publisher, Medina, OH, 1965

Smith, Larry D., editor, Kenneth J. Collins, Keith W. Drury, Richard S. Taylor and Wallace Thornton, Jr., *Counterpoint: Dialogue with Drury on The Holiness Movement*, Schmul Publishing Company, Shoals, IN. 2005

Snyder, Howard A., *The Radical Wesley: The Pattern and Practices of a Movement Maker*, Asbury Seedbed Publishing, Franklin, TN, (1996) 2014

The Wesleyan Discipline, Wesleyan Publishing House, Indianapolis, IN, 2016

Tozer, Aiden Wilson, *The Pursuit of God: The Human Thirst for the Divine*, Christian Publications, Harrisburg, PA, 1948

Walt, J.D., "The Second Half of the Gospel", video, seedbed.com, 2014

Watson, Kevin M. and Scott T. Kisker, *The Band Meeting: Rediscovering Relational Discipleship in Transformational Community*, Asbury Seedbed Publishing, Franklin, TN, 2017

Wiest, Jon, *Banding Together: A Practical Guide for Disciple Makers*, Wesleyan Publishing House, Indianapolis, IN, 2018

Wesley, John, *A Plain Account of Christian Perfection*, no publication information, c. 1885 (the personal copy belonging to my great-great-grandmother Mary Elizabeth Johnson, 1861-1950)

Wesley, John, *The Works of John Wesley*, Beacon Hill Press, Kansas City, 1979

Wigger, John H., *American Saint: Francis Asbury and the Methodists*, Oxford University Press, New York, NY, 2009

Wood, A. Skevington, *John Wesley: A Burning Heart*, William B. Eerdmans Publishing Company, Grand Rapids, 1967

Wynkoop, Mildred Bangs, *Theology of Love: The Dynamic of Wesleyanism*, Beacon Hill Press, Kansas City, 1972

OUTTAKES

Items that didn't make the cut.

The Pilgrim Holiness side of the family followed the other American Holiness Movement churches in establishing Bible Colleges to train workers (this was from the Second Coming influence among them). They added junior college programs later. Only Owosso offered a four-year liberal arts degree, I believe. The Pilgrim Holiness schools were strong on teaching the American Holiness Movement brand of understanding and living the sanctified life. They were training schools for holiness preachers and workers, primarily. The Wesleyan Methodists established liberal arts colleges with a Department of Religion embedded. When the merger took place in 1968, the newly formed denomination had ten colleges between them. There was Central Wesleyan College, Houghton College, Marion College, and Miltonvale Wesleyan College from the Wesleyan Methodist side, Eastern Pilgrim College, Frankfort Pilgrim College, Owosso College, Southern Pilgrim College, and Western Pilgrim College from the Pilgrim Holiness side, plus Bethany Bible College from the former Reformed Baptist Church in Canada. Since Bible colleges are difficult to sustain (their preacher alumni usually don't make a lot of money) and narrow in scope, the new denomination decided to keep open the Wesleyan Methodist schools and close the Pilgrim Holiness schools, with the exception of Western Pilgrim College (which became Bartlesville Wesleyan College then Oklahoma Wesleyan University), and the merged Allentown, Frankfort and Kernersville Bible colleges which became United Wesleyan College, but was soon discontinued. Bethany Bible College which is now Kingswood University is the only Bible college to survive. Currently, there are five Wesleyan schools of higher education: Houghton College, Indiana Wesleyan University, Kingswood University, Oklahoma Wesleyan University and Southern Wesleyan University. Wesley Seminary is the official seminary of the denomination, but it is organizationally embedded in Indiana Wesleyan University.

Is it going to be about me, or is it going to be about him and about them? Is it going to be for me, or is it going to be by me for him and for them?

How the Evangelical Movement Put Out the Wesleyan Fire
We had one job and we walked away from it. We were intended to be the victorious chicken that crossed the theological road to show the one-dimensional 'possum it could be done. But we opted to become a 'possum instead.

Anything that looked or smelled like "social gospel" was avoided like the plague. Two reasons: Jesus was coming back so we don't have time to waste on that, and that kind of thing was what the Liberals do and we're not Liberals.

Imago Dei

This theological concept undergirds much of Wesley's theological structure. It is the vestige of his education in classical theology, his growing up in the Church of England, and his fondness for the ancient fathers. His anthropology appears to be an understanding of the work of God in us to bring about the restoration of who we are created to be, but was lost in the fall. The image of God is partially but not perfectly restored through the works of grace of regeneration and sanctification. We are restored in form of character but not to the full pre-fallen Adamic likeness. In one stanza of "Hark! The Herald Angels Sing", Charles makes reference to "Adam's image now effaced." This concept is implied throughout American Holiness Movement theology as well but was almost totally absent from the public preaching of the doctrine.

Proverbs 4:23 is a key verse to the heart-centered theology of Wesley. "Above all else, guard your heart, for it is the wellspring of life." If it gets poisoned, your whole life is poisoned. If it gets cleansed, your whole life is cleansed.

"I continue to dream and pray about a revival of holiness in our day that moves forth in mission and creates authentic community in which each person can be unleashed through the empowerment of the Spirit to fulfill God's creational intentions." Compatible with Wesleyan thought, but is this really John Wesley? I am assured by some that it is, but I have trouble believing it.

Holiness Terminology

Holiness, Heart purity, Second blessing, Second definite work of grace, Deeper life, Deeper walk, Lordship of Christ, Total surrender, Total dedication, Total consecration, Baptism of the Holy Spirit, Filled with the Spirit, Exchanged life, Filled with the fullness of God, Perfect love, Christian perfection

---

"Without Holiness, no one will see the Lord." It became, "If you don't believe 'holiness' the way we believe it, you'll not make it to heaven." It completely missed the grace in the next verse, "See to it that no one misses the grace of God." Where did that arrogance (is that too strong a term?) come from? Not from the Father's heart. "The Lord ... is not willing that any should perish, but that all should come to repentance."

If God has a will and we have a will, whose will will prevail?

You won't find this by trying to figure out a formula. This is about a spirit of sacrifice and surrender, and moving in the direction of God. This is not about mastering the mystery. It's about living in sacrifice and surrender, and moving in the direction of God. There's an old adage that says, "You can't steer a parked car." Start rolling in the direction of God.

An elderly pastor said to me recently, "Dan, who do you think invented the mimeograph machine, God or the devil?" I responded, "I'm pretty sure the devil did, but what he meant for evil, God meant for good. It became a sanctifying agent for many of us!" For those who grew up with copy machines, you have no idea. No idea. If God cared about me being driven to tears by a machine that seemed to be possessed by demons, and would tenderly answer my prayer to please help me get this bulletin printed, then he is a good God who cares about even the trivial trials of his children.

Made in the USA
Middletown, DE
27 December 2018